PENSACOLA:
Spaniards to Space Age

By
Virginia Parks

Pensacola Historical Society
1986

The Pensacola Historical Society is a not-for-profit educational organization which operates the Pensacola Historical Museum in Old Christ Church. The Society is dedicated to the preservation of Pensacola and West Florida history and heritage through museum collections, monthly programs for its members and guests, and through publication of books and periodicals. Society programs are operated from public and private contributions with an Endowment Trust Fund for tax-deductible gifts and memorials (I.R.S. No. 59 0917279).

Cover design by Diane Dusevitch

Library of Congress Cataloging in Publication Data
    Pensacola : Spaniards to space age.

    Includes index.
    1. Pensacola (Fla.)--History. I. Title.
F319.P4P32 1986   975.9'99   86-2522
ISBN 0-939566-04-4

CONTENTS

ACKNOWLEDGMENTS

Sketching a history of Pensacola required the talent and assistance of many historians, editors, artists, friends and colleagues. Their work is on these pages. I am greatly indebted to all of them.

First of all, there is my editor: Sandra Johnson, assistant curator of the Pensacola Historical Museum. Her guiding hand, attention to detail, layout expertise and, most of all, her continuing encouragement led to the completion of the manuscript.

Jesse Earle Bowden, editor and vice-president of the *Pensacola News Journal* and president of the Pensacola Historical Society edited the first draft. His changes and additions added color to the story. I am also indebted to him for his inspiring introduction to the book.

Dianne Dusevitch, illustrator and design consultant, brightened the dust jacket with her artistic drawing. Her talent and knowledge of early Indians gave autenticity to her sketches of pre-historic Indian life.

Norman Simons, curator of the Pensacola Historical Museum, assisted in selecting the pictures and illustrations for the book. His familiarity with the photographic collections of the Pensacola Historical Society and the T. T. Wentworth Collection proved invaluable.

Many thanks are due Dr. William S. Coker and Dr. James R. McGovern, professors in the history department of the University of West Florida and Woodward B. Skinner, historian of the Pensacola Historical Society, whose professional skill and knowledge assured historical accuracy; Elizabeth Vickers, medical historian and good friend who kept my participles from dangling; James Major, who kept my commas straight and my "i's" dotted; Helen Hunt who educated me on the use of commas; Spencer Butts, Mary Veal and Sandy Reaves who helped make the manuscript understandable; and Claire LeMacher, assistant curator of the Pensacola Historical Society, who proof read the final draft.

A grant from the Gannett Foundation, through assistance by the *Pensacola News Journal*, assured the fulfillment of a long-time goal of the Pensacola Historical Society: a general history of the city for the enlightenment and pleasure of general readers and especially for students in West Florida schools.

And, a special thanks to my husband, Paul, for his patience, understanding and continuing encouragement during the past year.

Virginia Parks

Pensacola: Ever a Frontier

In the beginning there is the harbor:

Sun-bleached, wind-swept, its broad bay touched sand and sea; its dimensions defined by saltmarsh and swamp; bordered by bush and scrub, ancient oak and fan-fronded palmetto.

For centuries it's a haven for aboriginal nomads; fishing in streams, rivers and bays; living on sandy shores and red-clay cliffs; sharing fish and game and fruits of nature's endless cycle of pulsating life.

Peaceful, unspoiled . . . thousands of miles across uncharted waters from an awakening by Europeans who begin venturing from the confines of medieval geography and thought.

By the sixteenth century European seafarers and captains of colonization on exploratory voyages sail into the tranquil waters of the almost land-locked bay. They dream of gold and conquest and commerce. They carry flags of Spain with musket, Christian cross, sword and cannon. They stake claims for king and country.

La Florida.

And, now, Ochuse. In time, Panzacola.

The northern harbor of the Floridas is a touchstone of a New World north of the Caribbean, envisioned by lusting Conquistadors as a dusky, voluptuous goddess dressed in the riches of Magnificent Discovery — a map point on the Gulf of Mexico with lands beyond the bay ripe with the promise of an earthly paradise scarcely less fruitful than Eden itself.

Again and again they return, would-be conquerors from Europe:

Spaniards; then Frenchmen, battling for their own sandspit beachhead; the Spaniards again, clinging to their toehold with visions of continental destiny. Then the British, transforming the bayfront military stockade into a town. Panzacola, in the meager beginning; now, a town, Pensacola.

Yet the tenacious Spaniards return in anger and siege, storming the town, chasing the British from their sanctuary in the Gulf of Mexico as the fires of American independence elsewhere signal the destiny of North America.

Then, a nation aborning, the Americans — ending colonization spanning more than two centuries — arrive with the heavy bootprint of General Andrew Jackson, twice the town's conqueror — in 1814 and 1818 — and in 1821 the provisional governor of the Floridas under the flag of the United States.

Old Hickory, determined to snare the Spanish Floridas for the new, emerging nation, envisions great economic promise for Pensacola. He's encouraged by the harbor's potential as a major military defense position. He shares the same vision of colonials who claimed the same sands, sea and harbor.

Scene of Spanish Florida's origins, French occupation and British development and military defeat, Pensacola — the old colonial capital of West Florida — discovers a new destiny in 1825 when the U. S. Navy began a navy yard and depot on the harbor mainland. And, ringing the harbor, massive red-brick fortifications built by the Americans foretell Pensacola's place in the building of a nation.

Through three conflicts — Mexican War, Civil War and Spanish-American War — Pensacola's Navy Yard is the scene of military preparedness, ship-building, military attack and coastal defense.

Ever a frontier even today, Pensacola in its more than four centuries accumulated legacies of Spanish failure and military conquest, French colonial ambition, British townsmanship and colonial neglect, shattered Southern dreams, West Florida timber and lumber prosperity, city-building vision and economic decline, and the misfortunes of its geographic isolation in the westernmost corner of the long peninsula.

By the second decade of the twentieth century, Pensacola was again on the threshold of a new destiny as the spawning ground for the birth and nurturing of naval aviation.

Pensacola was the Deep Water City.

And the Cradle of Naval Aviation. And the Mother-in-law of the U. S. Navy.

In four foreign conflicts — World Wars I and II, the Korean Conflict and the nightmares of Vietnam and Southeast Asia — Pensacola paraded legions of Navy airmen earning their wings of gold. They were aloft as pioneers flying canvas-skinned Jennies sputtering over the historic bay; they were Space Age professionals in computerized cockpits of supersonic jets zooming off Pensacola runways and aircraft carrier decks.

From colonial exploration and intrigue to Americanization, from nineteenth century wooden sailing ships to the airborne technology of the aeronautic and space age, Old Pensacola retains its birthright as the original city of Florida's last frontier, West Florida.

In its long past, Pensacola and its historic harbor enriched the development of the American Gulf Coast. Today Pensacola preserves many of its landmarks as silent sentinels, echoes of its many generations of historical destiny. Yet, sharing with St. Augustine Florida's ancient origins, Pensacola echoes a new destiny and an unending adventure that began more than four centuries before the space age when Spaniards first saw what they described as the "best port in the Indies."

Jesse Earle Bowden

Editor and Vice-President
Pensacola News Journal

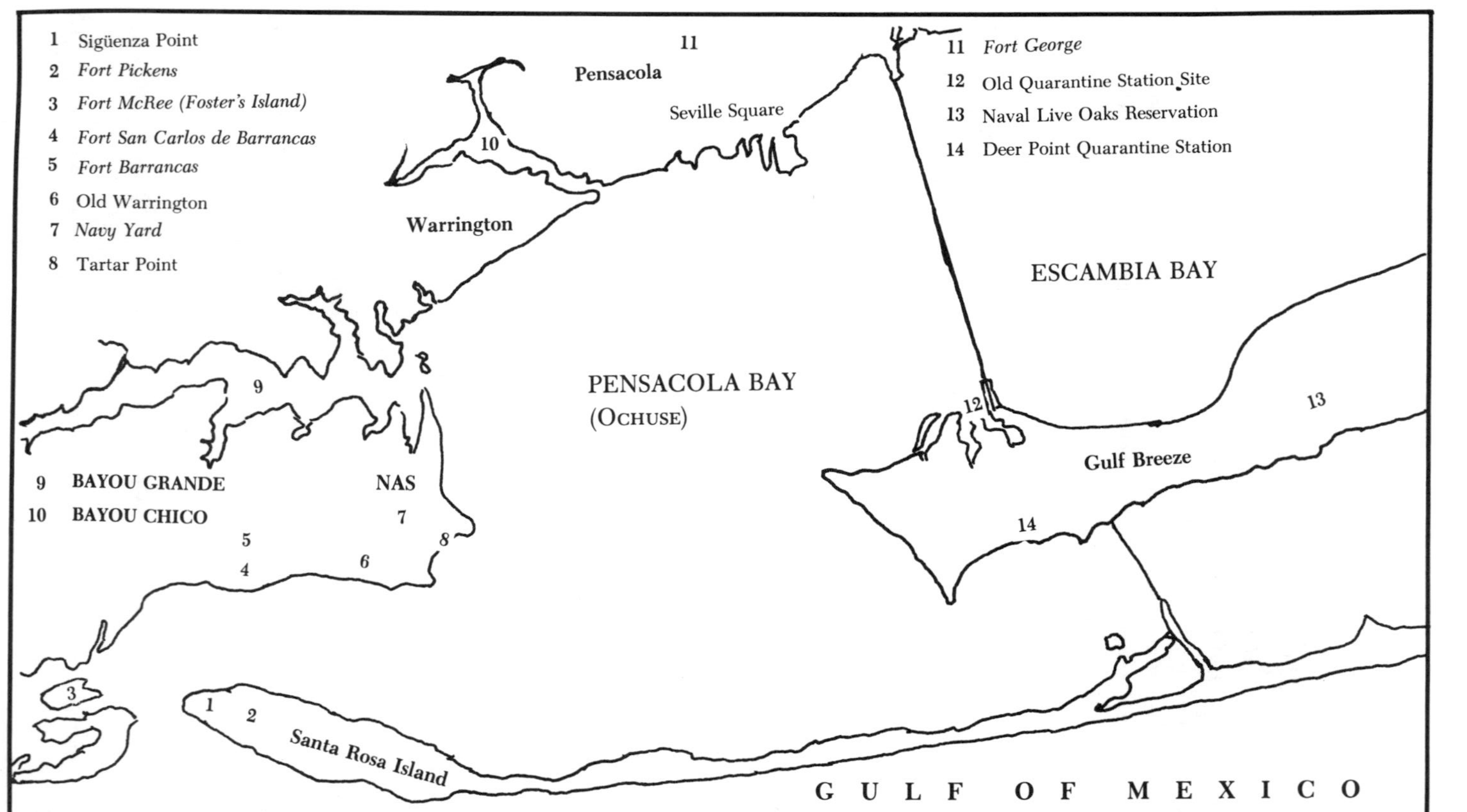

Points of Historical Interest in Pensacola Area.

Map by Sandra L. Johnson.

1 "MANY CANOES CAME TO GREET US"

As the last great Ice Age ended and the huge glaciers retreated northward, rivers, bays and bayous formed on the North American continent. One body of water left by the receding glaciers was a beautiful, almost land-locked, bay which came to be known as Pensacola Bay. The two barrier islands which still guard its narrow entrance rose from the sea. The soft, white sands along the shore came from the Appalachian Mountains as huge rocks were washed down through the rivers during an indeterminate length of time. The clear grains of sand were almost pure quartz and the resulting color resembled fresh-fallen snow.[1]

Thousands of years rolled by before the waters of the bay sank to their present levels. While the seas and their tributaries were still shrinking, the first Indians came to the shores of Pensacola Bay. The story of the earliest inhabitants of the land beside the bay has been literally "dug up" by archaeologists. Through examinations of archaeological sites, they have pieced—and are still piecing—together the development of an ancient people called by various cultural classifications: Paleo, Archaic, Deptford, Woodland, Mississippian and Fort Walton/Pensacola. Their story is one of evolvement through a long period of time from a wandering group totally occupied with hunting for food to a more settled people with an interest in family and tribal activities.

Nomadic bands of Paleo Indians who wandered into Florida following the last glacial age (9,000 - 7,000 B. C.) first inhabited the shores of Pensacola Bay. They were hunters who shifted camp sites frequently in the pursuit of herds of large animals. As the animals moved, so did the Indians. During the last part of the Paleo period, the herds of megafauna grazed near the Escambia River and, possibly, along Pensacola Bay. The Paleo Indians followed the game and, when that food supply was inadequate, they fished using hooks made from bone and chipped stone.[2]

As the centuries passed, the Indians learned more about their surroundings. Competition for available food from the herds increased and the people had to search for other sources for sustenance. Between

Archaeologists directed by Dr. Judith Bense at the University of West Florida put together fragments of a Deptford Period bowl. The pieces, excavated from the Hawkshaw site in 1985, form an almost complete bowl. Drawing by Dianne Dusevitch, design consultant, Hawkshaw Project.

6,000 and 2,000 B. C., the Archaic Period Indians supplemented their meat diet with plant food, fish and shellfish. As agricultural practices began to develop, the less nomadic people lived in temporary shelters made of natural fibers and wooden poles. To cook their food, they heated rocks and fired clay cooking balls which they dropped into skin-lined holes in the ground. Garbage heaps, known as shell middens, grew outside the rude homes. Toward the end of the Archaic Period, these ancient people developed the art of making pottery for cooking use. The changes and development in style and decoration of pottery types have been used by archaeologists to denote pre-historic Indian cultural periods.[3]

Deptford pottery was first discovered near Savannah, Georgia at a location called the Deptford site and the name describes a cultural period of Indian development. During the Deptford Period (1000 B. C. to 1 A. D.) coastal area population grew. The Indians lived in family groups in villages of five to ten homes with each dwelling housing five to ten people. Inland sites show that the people sometimes moved to the interior to gather nuts, fruits and berries. Most Deptford Period sites, however, existed along the coast or along rivers and bays where food was abundant. Some Indians lived along the northeastern shore of Pensacola Bay in an area known today as Hawkshaw. Their homes were simple lean-tos made from reeds or palmetto fronds which were attached to a wooden framework. The Hawkshaw camp, probably seasonal, was inhabited only in good fishing weather.[4]

The Santa Rosa Swift-Creek Period and the Weeden Island Period followed. Changes in pottery delineate the different Indian cultures and also reveal societal development. Villages became more permanent as agricultural practices advanced. Since the basic need for obtaining food was more easily satisfied, the Indians began to contemplate the world around them and to deal with philosophical questions. Important ceremonial and religious rites developed. The dead were interred in burial mounds along with tools, ornaments and pottery.[5]

Indians of the last pre-European period of Pensacola's history belonged to the Fort Walton and Pensacola Periods. The Pensacola Period was represented by the various tribes located along the coast west of Fort Walton. Included among these tribes were the Pensacola or Panzacola Indians.[6] These people had more leisure time than had their ancestors. They engaged in games such as stickball and gambled with gamestones. Their clothing was made of cloth as well as animal skins. Agricultural methods improved as tool technology advanced.[7] At this time, some Indians moved farther inland perhaps to take advantage of more fertile crop lands or because of population pressure.[8] Others remained in the bay area and these were the Indians who greeted the first Spanish explorers in Pensacola Bay.

Twenty-one years after Columbus' celebrated voyage of 1492 charted the course of exploration of lands unknown to Europeans, the Spaniard, Juan Ponce de Leon, was officially credited with the discovery of Florida. There is speculation other Spaniards "unofficially" found Florida before 1513. But Ponce de Leon capitalized on the discovery. In April 1513 his men sloshed ashore somewhere in the vicinity of St. Augustine. Ponce de Leon claimed the new land for the King of Spain and christened it La Florida. Following his landing

Deptford Period Indians lived by the shores of Pensacola Bay long before Spanish explorers discovered the harbor. Artist Dianne Dusevitch recreated their lifestyle based on research by University of West Florida Professor Judith Bense in the Hawkshaw region on the northeast shore of Pensacola Bay.

the Florida east coast, Ponce de Leon sailed first northward to the mouth of the St. Johns River and then turned southward. He rounded the Florida Keys and continued north into the Gulf before returning to his base in Puerto Rico.[9]

Sailing across uncharted waters and using primitive navigational instruments, other Spanish seamen continued to scout the long coastline of Florida. In 1516 the two Miruelos, uncle and nephew, may have been the first to sail into Pensacola Bay. The younger Miruelo later accompanied the expedition which was commissioned by Francisco de Garay, the governor of Jamaica. Alonso Alvarez de Pineda, Garay's agent, took four caravels to search the Gulf for a strait to the east. He failed to find that elusive water passage, but he did map the northern Gulf coast as far south as the Yucatan Peninsula, possibly entering Pensacola Bay during the course of his expedition.

In 1526 Lucas Vasquez de Ayllon explored the east coast and attempted to plant a settlement near the Cape Fear River in North Carolina. The stories of Santa Elena stemmed from this voyage. For years, the name Santa Elena conjured up visions of a fine harbor suitable for military fortification and settlement. Since it was thought to be on the same latitude as fertile northern Spain, the Spanish believed that the area could support an abundant crop just as in their homeland. The "Santa Elena complex" developed and thoughts of settlement in this supposedly lush land prompted other voyages. One of the primary reasons for Tristan de Luna's expedition to Pensacola was the discovery of Santa Elena, now thought to be Parris Island, South Carolina.[10]

The intrepid Spanish explorers kept probing the coast of Florida. In 1528 Panfilo de Narvaez landed near Tampa Bay and marched as far as Apalachee near present-day Tallahassee. Here, starving and discouraged, his sailors made boats of logs hoping to sail to Mexico. Hugging the coastline, the homemade fleet stopped several times for provisions. When they entered one of the bays along the northern Gulf Coast, two men, a Christian Greek named Teodoro and a friendly Indian or Negro, left the group to go with some Indians in search of water. The two men were never seen again. Years later members of the Soto* expedition found a dagger, a relic of Teodoro, in the region of Pensacola.[11]

---

*Traditionally, Spanish names do not carry the "de" when only the family name is used, i.e., Soto instead of de Soto is the accepted version.

The treasurer of the Narvaez expedition, Cabeça de Vaca, described the Indians of the area as being "of large stature and well-formed. . ." They lived by the shoreline in dwellings made of mats and cooked fish in clay pots. Cabeça de Vaca also noted the supply of fresh water probably because the Narvaez men had been without water for five days. The Spaniards were lulled into a false sense of security by the fact that the Indians had no bows and arrows. During the night the Indians attacked the men of the Narvaez expedition with stones and drove them from the shores of Pensacola Bay.[12]

These explorations of the Florida coastline led to the major expedition of Hernando De Soto in 1539 — an expedition which later had great influence on plans to colonize Pensacola. Soto landed near Tampa and marched northward. While the main body of explorers paused to rest at Apalachee, Soto sent three small expeditions to explore the surrounding territory. Diego Maldonado led one of these parties into Pensacola Bay. When he returned to Apalachee, he told of the magnificent bay. Soto sent Maldonado to Havana for more provisions and ordered the captain to meet the main party in Pensacola during the summer of 1540.

Maldonado returned to Pensacola on several occasions waiting for the main body of the expedition to arrive. They never did. Soto had marched north and west from Apalachee, finally reaching the "Province of Coosa" in July 1540. A recent archaeological expedition located the province of Coosa in an area stretching from northeast Alabama through northwest Georgia and into Tennessee.[13] A chronicler of the expedition, known only as "The Gentleman of Elvas," wrote that this land was well watered and more densely populated than any other place he had yet seen. The Indians were friendly; the chief even invited the Spaniards to settle in Coosa. Soto declined and decided to continue to march westward towards the Mississippi River which he named the *Río Grande de la Florida*.[14]

The narrative of the Gentleman of Elvas contained lavish praise for the land of Coosa. Other survivors of the Soto expedition called Florida "a land full of bogs and poisonous fruits, barren, and the very worst country that is warmed by the sun."[15] Future colonists paid much attention to the description of Coosa and probably agreed with the description of Florida.

2 "A Man Zealous In Our Service . . ."

Even though the explorers wrote of the fine bay on the northern Gulf coast, Spain exhibited little interest until the middle of the sixteenth century. Silver from New Spain (Mexico) was far more interesting to King Philip II and his viceroy. Each year, the great treasure galleons, laden with precious metals for the coffers of Spain, churned eastward across the Caribbean Sea and the Atlantic Ocean. The flat and sandy land around the fabulous bay, then called Ochuse, could not begin to compete with the mines of Mexico.

Finally, spurred by rumors of French colonization plans, the desire of the Catholic Church to establish missions in Florida and the need for a haven for treasure ships threatened by hurricanes and pirates, King Philip II issued a Royal *Cédula* to the Viceroy of Mexico, Luis de Velasco. Told to pick a leader who "shall seem suitable to you, one fearful of God our Lord and zealous in our service," Velasco promptly chose Don Tristan de Luna y Arellano.[1]

A member of the old Luna family of Borobia in Castille, Don Tristan was the younger brother of the head of the house, Don Pedro. Since Don Pedro had no sons, his brother was the sole heir to estates which yielded an annual revenue of three million maravedis and the title of Mariscal of Castille. These prospects of good fortune made him a highly desirable leader of an expedition costing vast sums of money. Other qualifications included his almost thirty years of loyal service in the New World.

As a young man eager for adventure, Don Tristan first came to New Spain with Cortez in 1519. Later, he rode with the Coronado expedition into New Mexico as a cavalry officer, rising to the position of Maestro de Campo (Chief of Staff). He was in ill health when he returned to Mexico City and seemingly had had enough of exploration. In 1545 Don Tristan married the twice widowed Dona Isabel de Rojas. She brought her inheritances from both husbands to her new marriage. Dona Isabel died before Don Tristan's appointment as Governor of Florida. She left her estates in trust to their two legitimate children and the income from the estates to Don Tristan who was engaged in various forms of civil and military service. When he was appointed to lead the

Spanish soldiers of Tristan de Luna's time wore protective armor. From left to right: a horseman, an arquebusier, a sergeant, a captain (on horseback) and a lancer. Picture from Harold L. Peterson, *Arms and Armor in Colonial America* (U. S. A.: Bramwell House Division of Clarkson N. Potter, Inc. by arrangement with Stackpole Co., 1956).

expedition, he had just finished quelling an Indian rebellion in Oaxaca. In addition to this military experience, his income could and would be used to help finance a colonization attempt.

Tristan de Luna was a logical choice for the position of Governor General of Florida and leader of the expedition. Greatly esteemed by his contemporaries in New Spain, he "lived as a very upright gentleman, setting a good example in his person as a very worthy Christian, a man of clean life and a servant of His Majesty."[2] It was said of him that "the presidents, judges, governors, and viceroys who have been here have esteemed and honored him for the character and goodness of his person, as also have caballeros, hidalgos, and other persons . . ."[3]

As the most ambitious and well planned of the Spanish ventures in the New World, the expedition "contemplated the establishment of permanent Spanish bases in the indefinite region called 'Florida' . . . both on the Atlantic and Gulf sides."[4] This concept was a notable departure from the "Gold and God" mission which had governed previous expeditions. For the first time Spain embarked upon a colonization attempt rather than an expedition of exploration and conversion of the heathen.

Luna selected Maldonado's Bay of Achusi (Ochuse) as the site of the base on the northern Gulf coast. He planned to include artisans, farming settlers, women and some Indians in the complement of the expedition. These 1,000 civilians would be protected by 500 soldiers. A large group of friars would emphasize the missionary character of the enterprise. Provisions consisted of arms, tools, corn, biscuit, bacon, drief beef, cheese, oil, vinegar and wine. Horses and some live cattle were included in the expedition; the settlers hoped to breed the animals when they arrived at Achusi.

On June 11, 1559, Don Tristan de Luna y Arellano and the members of the expedition boarded thirteen ships at Vera Cruz, Mexico. They set sail for the Bay of Achusi, a voyage normally of less then two weeks. It lasted for sixty-three days. Unpredictable Gulf storms blew the fleet off course to Florida's lower west coast. Supplies for the first part of the colonization attempt were either consumed or lost; many horses died during the storm. Eventually, the ships were able to sail northwest and finally entered the bay of Achusi on August 14, 1559.[5]

Since August 15 was the day of the Ascension of the Queen of Angels (Mother Mary) into Heaven, Luna named the bay Santa María. To pay homage to the king, he added the name Filipina. Thus Pensacola Bay was given its first modern name: Bahía Filipina del Puerto de Santa María. Luna glowingly described the bay in a report to King Philip:

> Seamen say that it is the best port in the Indies, the town and the site which has been selected for founding is no less good, for it is a high point of land which slopes down to the bay where the ships come to anchor. Concerning the country, I have up to now learned no secret. It seems to be healthy. It is somewhat sandy, from which I judge that it will not yield much bread. There are pine trees, live-oaks, and many other kinds of trees.[6]

No one knows exactly where the Luna party landed. Speculation has centered on the high ground near present day Fort Barrancas or on the bluffs near the entrance to Bayou Texar. The only location given by Luna was that the camp was made on a high point of land which commanded a view of the anchorage. Here, he decided to erect a town supporting eighty to one hundred people. Some colonists would defend the port; others were ordered inland to seek subsistence from the Indians which would save expenses as well as ensure safety.[7]

Supplies were the first concern. Due to the long passage and the storm at sea, the colonists found themselves desperately short on food. Two parties went inland in search of friendly Indians and food. The remaining provisions were left aboard ships which were to be used as shelter until suitable huts were erected. Before the search parties returned, disaster struck the anchored fleet.

On Monday, the nineteenth of August, a hurricane blew into Pensacola Bay. The fierce storm raged for twenty-four hours and "did irreparable damage to the ships of the fleet. [There was] great loss by many seamen and passengers, both of their lives as well as of their property. All the ships which were in port went aground (although it is one of the best ports there are in the Indies), save only one caravel and two barks. . . ."[8]

With the loss of supplies, food became the paramount concern. One of the surviving ships was immediately sent to New Spain with news of the disaster and to bring back supplies. Unfortunately, the Luna expedition had taken virtually all the supplies when it departed. The rainy season had begun and all supplies had to be transported by mule from the interior to the coast. The Viceroy appealed to Havana for help, but the food situation was also critical in Cuba. Few ships were

Pensacola artist Herbert Rudeen's watercolor painting of the Luna landing on the shores of Pensacola Bay depicts sailors, soldiers and friars in the colonization group. The original painting hangs in the Pensacola Historical Museum. Pensacola Historical Society photo.

available and no surplus crops had been planted. Velasco recommended that Luna move inland to find food and promised that supplies would arrive in March or April.[9]

Meanwhile, Luna sent a food-seeking expedition under the command of Sergeant Major Mateo del Sauz to locate the Indian town of Nanipacana, mentioned by the Gentleman of Elvas in his narrative of the Soto expedition. Sauz marched northwest and found a few Indian settlements on the Alabama River. Nanipacana, consisting of eighty huts, was the largest of these villages. Although the Indians fled at the approach of the Spaniards, they left supplies of corn and beans. This good news was sent back to Luna.

At Ochuse Luna resettled, fearing that he would miss the promised relief ships if he joined the Sauz party. He also became ill the first of several disabling attacks which were to strike him during stressful times. Sauz continued to urge him to move to Nanipacana, but the leader remained hestitant. His indecision greatly affected the morale of the people under his command. When he finally decided to move to Nanipacana, supplies at the Indian town were exhausted.

Once again, Sauz traveled north — to Coosa this time — on a food-finding mission. His hungry men resented marching away from the promised relief ships. Once they arrived at Coosa, they decided the area was unfit for planting and harvesting. Although Sauz may have agreed with his men, he did not want to make the decision to abandon Coosa by himself and urged Luna to join him in Coosa.

At Nanipacana, Luna dealt with starving, demoralized and almost mutinous troops. Again he was ill; again he refused to make decisions. Married troops petitioned the leader to send their families home. They were soon joined by many others in the desire to escape from hardship by returning to New Spain. Finally, Luna consented to a move back to Ochuse where relief ships finally arrived. Disappointment reigned when it was discovered that they carried scanty supplies. The sick and the non-combatants were sent home in these ships, at least reducing somewhat the demand on the short supply of food.[10]

After one year in Florida two-thirds of the original expedition disappeared. Of the 360 people at Ochuse only fifty were effective soldiers. Two hundred men were in Coosa. The remainder of the 1,500 original colonists either died or were sent back to Mexico. Luna lost control of his command through illness, hesitancy and stubborness. He was even briefly barred by the friars from attending mass. When he attempted to comply with an order to march overland to Santa Elena, he was rebuffed; the people refused to obey him.

Viceroy Velasco, realizing a replacement was paramount for salvaging the expedition, appointed Angel de Villafane. Possibly because of his friendship with Luna, the viceroy gave Luna the option of giving his accounting of the failure of the expedition in New Spain rather than in Spain.

Villafane arrived at Ochuse on March 16, 1561, with fresh soldiers and supplies. On April 9 he assumed the governorship and gave Luna license to return to Spain. Luna asked for and received permission to go by way of Havana.

Leaving a small detachment to hold Ochuse, Villafane sailed for Santa Elena. Once again, storms thwarted the mission; the fabled Santa Elena was not found. The men at Ochuse were finally evacuated and Pensacola remained undisturbed by Europeans for over one hundred and twenty years.[11]

Don Tristan de Luna had been destroyed by nature, famine and his own indecision. His illnesses must also be cited as a cause of the failure. Luna died in Spain, not entirely absolved of blame for the failure of the Pensacola settlement.

3 "The Indians Call This Bay Panzacola"

The great European powers ignored the fine harbor of Ochuse for almost 125 years following Luna's failure to establish a permanent settlement at Pensacola. Interest in the northern Gulf coast slowly emerged in the latter part of the seventeenth century. Now, England, France and Spain realized the strategic importance of this unsettled coastline. To England, the southeast was an inviting woodland, a place to obtain furs and Indian slaves.[1] To France, the southeast represented a potential empire between her Canadian and Caribbean colonies. To Spain, Florida was a great wilderness buffer that protected the silver mines of Mexico and Caribbean shipping.[2]

In 1684 Martín de Echagaray, a former naval captain and a resident of St. Augustine, revitalized Spanish interests in Pensacola. St. Augustine was founded in 1565, and, unlike Pensacola, endured. Echagaray proposed a search for another legendary bay (the Spaniards always seemed to be searching for elusive bays which may or may not have existed but which always offered the hope of riches and conquest). This time the bay was called Espíritu Santo and was supposed to lie along the northern Gulf coast somewhere between Apalachee and Tampico.

Echagaray's dream received tacit approval because the Spanish government panicked over the actions of Don Diego de Peñalosa, the deposed Spanish governor of New Mexico. Peñalosa, a renegade defector to France, hoped to convince Louis XIV to conquer the reportedly rich southwestern provinces of Quivira and Teguayo. When nothing resulted from the Peñalosa plan, Echagaray's scheme for finding Espíritu Santo was not accepted, yet it opened the Spanish mind to further exploration of the northern Gulf coast.[3]

During this time the Windward Squadron, a fleet of armed Spanish naval vessels, patrolled the Gulf of Mexico in order to protect the merchant fleet. Each year, the Spanish treasure fleet took gold and silver from Mexican and South American mines back to Spain. The treasure ships offered tempting targets to pirates, and the Windward Squadron ensured safe passage of the Gulf.

Fear of French conquest gave added impetus to Spanish interest and exploration of the coast. The Spanish government first heard of the probable existence of a French colony somewhere on the northern Gulf coast when the Windward Squadron captured a pirate vessel. One of the prisoners, a French boy, Denis Thomas, claimed he had been a member of a French colonial expedition which was to establish a colony at a place called Micippi. The boy had sailed from France on the LaSalle expedition but jumped ship in French Santo Domingo. Hoping to return to France, he shipped aboard the pirate vessel. Thomas' story alarmed the Spanish.

In 1684 French adventurer Sieur de la Salle sailed from LaRochelle with 300 settlers to establish a colony at the mouth of the Mississippi River. He was delayed at Hispaniola (Santo Domingo) by illness and shortage of supplies. The boy, Denis Thomas, could easily have been a member of that expedition. When LaSalle continued his voyage, he sailed past the mouth of the Mississippi River and established a short-lived colony at Garcitas Creek off Matagorda Bay on the Texas coast. The settlement failed when LaSalle was assassinated and the colonists massacred by Indians.[4]

Failure of the French colonization attempt was unknown to the Spanish. Following the capture of Denis Thomas, Admiral Palacios of the Windward Squadron recommended to the viceroy in Mexico City that an expedition be sent from Havana to locate the French colony and to locate Espíritu Santo. Between 1685 and 1690, no less than eleven Spanish expeditions set out to find the elusive French.[5] Finally, in 1689 they discovered the ruined site of the LaSalle settlement.

Although the point of all these Spanish expeditions was to find the LaSalle camp, one of the early voyages had enormous impact on the future of Pensacola Bay. In 1683 Admiral Palacios appointed Juan Enríques Barroto to be the leader of this expedition and Antonio Ramirez, a pilot of the Windward Squadron, to be his assistant. Juan Jordán de Reina, a subordinate officer, kept a log of the voyage. He described Pensacola Bay as the most beautiful bay he had ever seen and also used the name Panzacola:

> "... About 11 o'clock I saw a bay, the best I have ever seen in my life. We put into it, finding a depth of eight, nine, and ten fathoms at its entrance which is not very wide; after steering northwest, north and northeast inside the bay, I anchored in seven fathoms. Its opening lies almost north and south; the Indians call this bay Panzacola ... With the In-

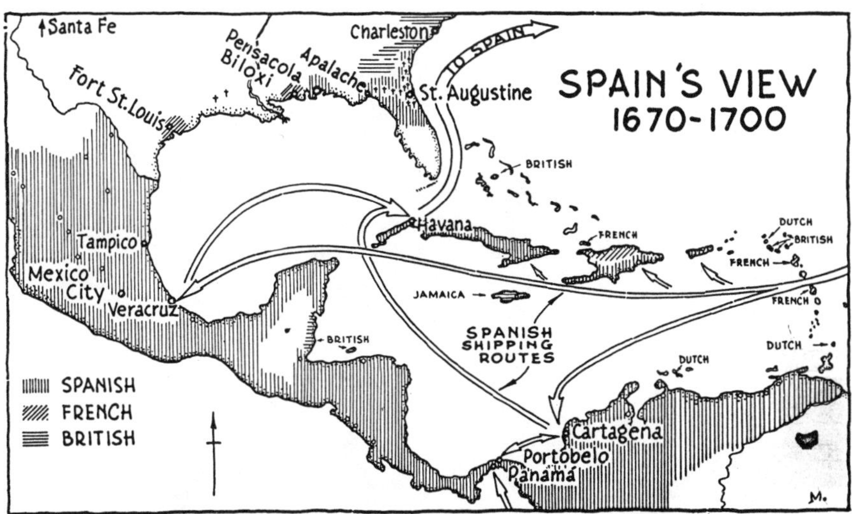

The Windward Squadron defended the Spanish shipping routes from the New World to Spain from pirates who preyed on the treasure ships. Map from Florida Historical Quarterly, 37, nos. 3 & 4 (Jan.-Apr. 1959). 224.

dian pilot we went in the longboat to the village of the Panzacola . . ."[6]

The Barroto expedition found Pensacola Bay on February 6, 1686. Jordán said it was thirty-six leagues from Apalachicola. The discovery and strategic location of the bay started an international race for its possession between France, Great Britain and Spain. The race was a slow one, however. The French were perhaps more interested in the Mississippi area; the British had a vested interest in colonies to the north; the Spanish procrastinated. It was not until June 26, 1692, that the King of Spain ordered the Viceroy of New Spain, Condé de Galve, to implement the plan by Admiral Andres de Pez to explore Pensacola

Mathematician and geographer Dr. Carlos de Sigüenza y Góngora mapped Pensacola Bay, named many of its prominent sites and wrote valuable descriptions of Indian life along the shores of the bay. Pensacola Historical Society photo.

Bay. Galve sent Pez with two vessels from Vera Cruz to Pensacola. Dr. Carlos de Sigüenza y Góngora, a mathematician and geographer, was a member of the expedition.

When Pez' ships reached Pensacola Bay on April 7, 1693, Sigüenza wrote:

> As soon as I saw the beauty and depth of its entrance, and the breadth and capacity of the inlet began to reveal itself, it occurred to me that this was the very port found by a pilot named Miruelo shortly after the discovery of America . . . And it was in search of this same port that Pánfilo de Narváez, accompanied by another pilot named Miruelo and a relative of the first, came on this ill-fated journey . . . I surmised, also, that this was the port called *Achusi* which, at the order of Hernando de Soto, adelantado of Florida, Captain Diego Maldonao sought and found . . . All this recalled to my mind, too, that this was the same bay to which Marshal Don Tristán de Luna y Arellano came . . .[7]

Once again, the bay was given a new name: Bahia de Santa María de Galve.[8] Sigüenza mapped the bay and its shores. He named the most prominent sites: Sigüenza Point on Santa Rosa Island and San Carlos on the west side of the bay. These two points guarded the entrance to the bay.[9]

Sigüenza explored the area surrounding the bay and left a detailed report of Indian life.

> . . . we found a fire burning over which was a very tasteless stew of buffalo entrails in a crudely shaped earthen pan, and the flesh of the same animal roasted, or rather singed in some places and raw in others, on some spits made of sticks; some fishes like dogfish were being roasted on others. In several baskets made of *otate* (a hard and solid reed) there were squash seeds and corn; in buckskin bags, the hair of buffaloes and other animals, mussel shells, bones, roots, and other odds and ends; . . . They had a little iron hatchet with the handle reversed, and small crosses made of reeds were found . . . Because of the thread and bunches of buffalo hair attached to them . . . I came to the conclusion that there was nothing mystical about them except that they served as spindles or distaffs for the women.[10]

At another site, Sigüenza noted additional facts about Indian life along the shores of the bay.

> A medium sized fishing craft was drawn up on the beach, and inside were an indefinite number of bows and arows: these were not made of reeds but of a shaft of hard wood tipped with bone. A little farther off was another boat, old and worm-eaten, with masts inside—indications that the Indians had come to this place for water.[11]

Both Sigüenza and Pez favored immediate settlement of the area. On June 13, 1694, the king issued a royal *cédula* ordering the viceroy to begin occupation of Pensacola. There was, however, little money available to finance the venture and, when the viceroy died in 1696, the project languished.

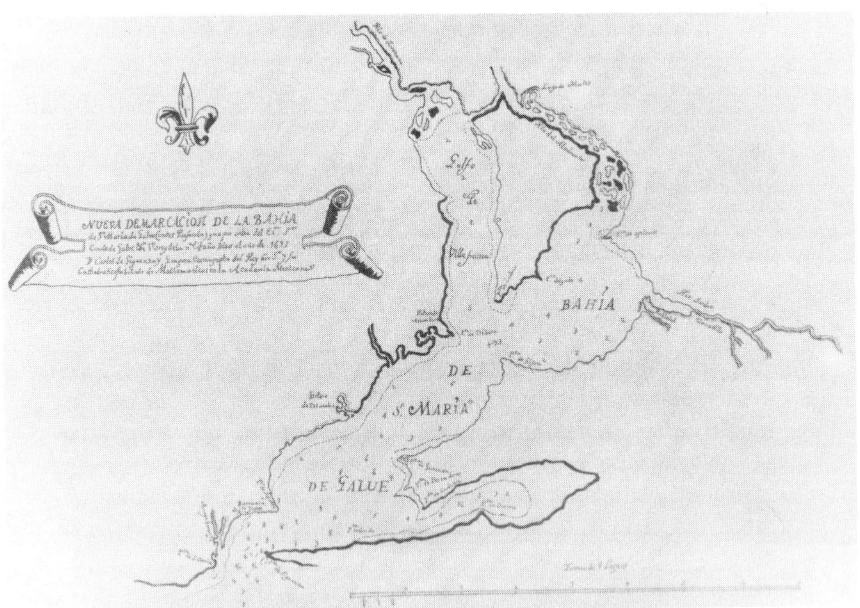

Dr. Carlos de Sigüenza sketched Bahia de Santa María de Galve in 1693. His map was probably used by the Arriola expedition which permanently settled Pensacola. Pensacola Historical Society photo.

4   "The Finest Jewel . . ."

"I hereby assert that that bay is the finest jewel possessed by his Majesty . . . may God protect him! . . . not only here in America but in all his kingdoms, because it combines the separate virtues that make other bays great." So wrote Don Carlos de Sigüenza in 1693.[1] But, despite this glowing report, the Spanish wavered in their interest in Pensacola.

Once again, reports of French and English expeditions destined for the northern coast of the Gulf of Mexico galvanized Spain into action. In 1698 France and Britain readied ships for expeditions into Gulf waters. The new viceroy, the Count of Moctezuma, received a Royal *Cédula* dated April 19, 1698, ordering him to dispatch a Spanish expedition for the purpose of occupying Pensacola Bay immediately.[2] The Spanish reasoned that even a weak hold on the bay would prove to be an effective barrier against the French and English. Indeed, Spanish priority in the occupation of the bay would later help to determine the boundary line between French Louisiana and Spanish Florida.[3]

The Royal *Cédula* reached Mexico on July 14, 1698. The viceroy immediately called upon two experts to plan the project: Andrés de Arriola and Dr. Carlos de Sigüenza y Góngora. Logistical plans for the settlement included the assembling of men for three expeditions. The Count of Moctezuma was directed to send as many men as possible to Pensacola. Martín de Arranguen Zavala, who had been sent from Cavite in the Philippines to Havana to check on overdue treasure ships, received orders to proceed from Havana to Vera Cruz to command the first expedition. Juan Jordán de Reina, then in Spain, received orders to rendezvous with Zavala in Havana to requisition troops and supplies. Jordán sailed from Havana on November 6, 1698. He reached Pensacola on November 17, four days ahead of the Vera Cruz expedition.[4]

When Arriola arrived at Pensacola on November 21, the troops and supplies were immediately landed at the *Barranca de Santo Tomé* (the present site of Fort Barrancas). Within six days, temporary quarters had been built and construction of Pensacola's first fort began. Jaime Franck, an Austrian who was considered to best military engineer in the New World, accompanied the Vera Cruz expedition. He was sixty

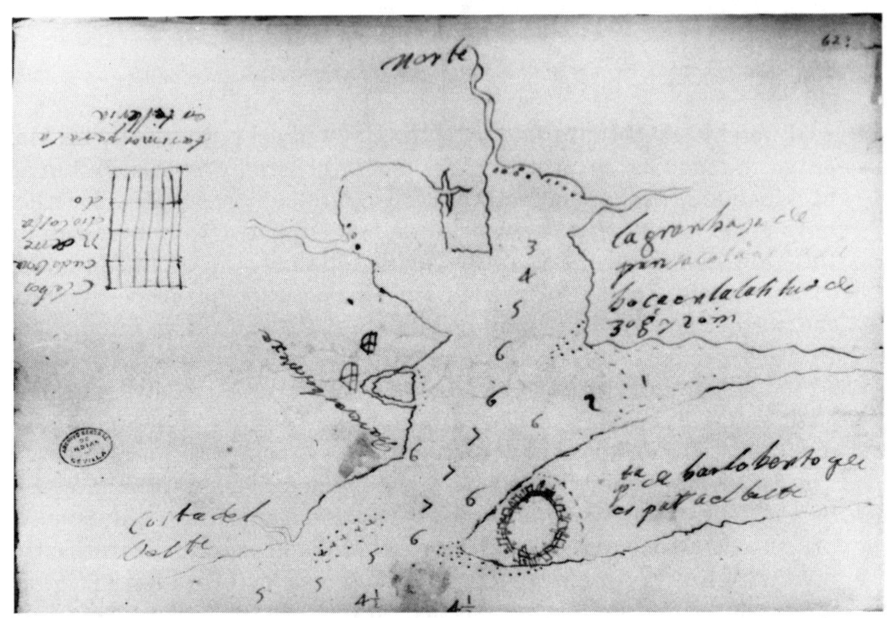

Jaime Franck, an Austrian military engineer, sketched Santa María de Galve (Pensacola Bay) in 1698 indicating the proposed Spanish fortifications, shows the island, the settlement area as well as the upper reaches of the bay. Original photo from Florida Historical Quarterly, *37, nos. 3 & 4 (Jan.-Apr. 1959), 233.*

years old and had sought retirement in Spain. But, permission was refused; he was ordered to Pensacola. His orders emphasized the high priority of the Pensacola settlement to Spain.[5]

The expedition included a few friars, almost 300 infantrymen and a labor battalion of black criminals who were to build the fort. The site selected, a high red clay bank on the mainland, soon received the name of *"Las Barrancas"* or more simply, "Barrancas." Since no stone existed in the area, the fort had to be constructed of wood. It was named for Charles, the second son of Leopold I, Emperor of Austria and

Hungary. The fourteen-year-old Charles or Carlos was considered by many people the heir apparent to the Spanish throne. Arriola, for some reason, named the fort San Carlos de Austria instead of Fort Carlos de Austria. The name was later perpetuated when the Hotel San Carlos was built in 1910.[6] Fort San Carlos de Austria, made of pine logs with four bastions and parapets of sand fill, had eighteen cannon (8-pounders and 10-pounders) that "peered out from the sandy crest of the bluff."[7] These cannon lacked the range to control the 3,000 foot-wide channel between Barrancas and Santa Rosa Island. Another battery on Sigüenza Point could work in conjunction with the San Carlos battery, providing a withering cross-fire through the channel. Although recommended by Sigüenza when he charted the bay, this battery was never constructed since the military officers reported that the point consisted "of shifting sand at sea level, all watery and drowned so that no fortification can be set there; because in heavy rains it is drowned, and when the south and southeast winds do blow the sea drowns it likewise."[8]

Pensacola's climate soon took its toll on the wooden Fort San Carlos as strong winds and constantly shifting sands undermined the structure. By 1700 the logs of the fort were already rotting. In 1702 the fort's commander, Don Francisco Martínez, said the structure was hardly worth calling a fort. It consisted "solely of a quadrangle of logs which would serve only as a stepping-over place for the enemy."[9]

Yet, other building was in progress. By 1701 Arriola established a hospital staffed by two surgeon-friars. The construction of the hospital came none too soon. In 1702 a severe epidemic decimated the population. Both medicine and hospital space were at a premium. The government had to buy at least one of the wooden houses owned by a soldier for additional hospital space.[10]

The settlers were beginning to confront Pensacola's perennial problems: hostile Indians; configuration and infertility of the soil; infrequent arrival of supply ships; and, always, the climate. In June 1700 Jaime Franck said the climate and the land were highly overrated. Pensacola would only waste the funds of the Royal Treasury and would shorten the days of those who lived in such a climate.[11]

In spite of attempts to produce food locally, Pensacola depended on the annual subsidy from New Spain. When the subsidy failed to arrive on time — frequently the case — the garrison traded with French Mobile even though such trade was illegal under French and Spanish law. In spite of this arrangement and relief shipments from St. Augustine and

Apalachee, the garrison was sometimes reduced to eating acorns and roots.

When food was available, the Spanish soldier existed on a ration of eight ounces of bread or corn and eight ounces of meat. Salt water was used for seasoning. This diet plus the climate gave Pensacola the reputation as a place of horror in New Spain. There were billets for 220 infantrymen, but the full complement was rarely achieved. Continuous recruitment in New Spain produced few volunteers. In 1712 the total population around Pensacola Bay totalled 212 including twenty-five women.

The presence of women had been scarce from the beginning of the settlement. No women arrived with the 1698 expedition. In the spring of 1704 four Spanish families and a few Apalachee Indians came to Pensacola. These may have been Pensacola's first female settlers since the aborted Luna expedition. Officials in New Spain were reluctant to send women to the garrison outpost for moral reasons.[12]

The caliber of both soldier and laborer remained low. Convicts who were recruited in Vera Cruz to perform the work of laborers often became disciplinary problems. Some of them set fire to the buildings in an attempt to force evacuation. Forty convicts deserted to the interior, but they soon returned. Even Pensacola was preferable to capture by hostile Indians.

The Creek Indians, supported by the British, attacked the small fort and settlement many times. In August 1707 they burned the houses outside of the fort. Later in the year the Indians again besieged the fort. In desperation, Spanish officers issued arms to the convicts as the number of soldiers had dwindled due to disease and conflicts with the hostile Indians. Luckily for the Spanish, the British withdrew their support and the fort held.[13]

Arriola continually petitioned New Spain for more money for defense. He and Jaime Franck realized that Fort San Carlos was totally inadequate to repel any concerted attack. Succeeding garrison commanders continued to beg for replacement of the rotting timbers of Fort San Carlos and for at least a battery at Point Sigüenza. Succeeding viceroys continued to refuse to allocate money for the erection of such a battery.[14]

The small settlement maintained a precarious hold upon the land. Rotting timbers, fleas and other insects, and the pervasive heat sapped the strength of both the fort and the garrison. These weaknesses were soon to be exposed by the French.

5 "And Captured This Place . . ."

For the first two decades of Spanish settlement in Pensacola, relations with the French in Mobile were cordial but wary. When the Mobile colony began in 1702, the Spanish Governor of Pensacola paid a call upon his French counterpart to protest the settlement. On the return voyage the Governor was shipwrecked. After abandoning his boat, he walked back to his French hosts who wined and dined their Spanish guest and sent him home in a French ship. Similar incidents indicate that the two colonies maintained friendly relations. Each helped the other with food and some trade existed between them. The settlers of the two communities had a common bond: survival in a frontier area.[1]

The cordial relations suddenly deteriorated in 1718 when Austria, Holland, France and England signed a treaty called the Quadruple Alliance. Great Britain declared war on Spain in December 1718; France followed suit in January 1719. The Mobile French learned of the declaration of war on April 13. Jean Baptiste LeMoyne and the Sieur de Bienville, brothers and leaders of the Mobile colony, promptly organized an expedition to capture Pensacola.[2]

The Spanish settlement was small. It consisted of 370 people; the governor and garrison of the fort comprised 307 of the total number. Fort San Carlos was crumbling with nine of its twenty-eight guns out of order. A small stockade had been built on Point Sigüenza along with a few huts for the laborers.[3] On May 14 the French fleet appeared off Santa Rosa Island, taking the Spanish by surprise. Three days later the French fleet sailed into the bay and exchanged shots with Fort San Carlos. The French captured the dunes above the fort and Governor Juan Pedro Matamoras surrendered.[4]

Another of Bienville's brothers, Lemoyne de Chateagué, became the commandant of Pensacola with a garrison of two hundred and fifty troops augmented by forty clerks and laborers. Although certain the Spanish would try to retake Pensacola, the French were not prepared for the assault when it occurred.[5]

Under the terms of capitulation the French had transported the entire Spanish garrison to Cuba in French ships. There, the Governor of

Battery San Antonio and Fort Barrancas. Pensacola Historical Society Photo.

Cuba ordered the French vessels seized and the crews made prisoners of war. The Spanish then used the two French ships as decoys to retake Pensacola. They sailed easily into Pensacola Bay and demanded the French surrender. At first the French refused, but after two days of ineffectual cannonade they agreed. The French left Pensacola, and the Spanish began to erect a stronger battery on Point Sigüenza and to build a small stockade to protect Fort San Carlos from a land attack.[6]

Once again the French sailed back into Pensacola Bay and captured Fort San Carlos in September 1719. This time they were not as polite as in the previous invasion. They burned the village and blew up Fort San Carlos. Nothing remains of the original fort. An inscription on the ruins of old Fort San Carlos reads: "In the year 1719, on the 18th day of September, Monsieur Desnard de Champmeslin, Commander of His Most Christain Majesty, captured this place and the Island of Santa Rosa by force of arms."[7]

Peace was restored among the great powers of Europe in 1720, but the fate of Pensacola still hung in the balance. After lengthy negotiations between Spain and France, Pensacola was finally restored to Spain. The two countries signed a treaty of alliance in which France forever renounced Pensacola and both kings agreed to be allies against Great Britain. The Spanish returned to Pensacola in 1722 and the last Frenchman left in 1723.[8]

6 STORMS AND HIGH TIDES

When the Spanish returned to Pensacola Bay in 1722, they were once again faced with the task of beginning a settlement. A bake oven and a lidless cistern were all that remained of Fort San Carlos.[1] Lieutenant Colonel Alejandro Wauchope was directed to supervise the rebuilding of the town and its fortifications. Wauchope, following the commands of his superiors, ordered the construction of a new fort at *Punta de Sigüenza* on Santa Rosa Island. He chose a site three-fourths of a mile east of Point Sigüenza and within one hundred yards of the island's north coast. It was built on piles driven deep into the sand and was designed to hold 150 men. Some bark roofed cabins stood within the stockade and others were erected outside of the fort.[2]

The outer cabins represented the beginning of a new town on Santa Rosa Island. By 1723 the stockade and the new town consisted of a paymaster's office, two barracks, a house for the captain, a powder magazine, twenty-four small buildings, eight larger homes, a cook oven and a lookout tower.[3]

The island settlement remained a garrison town dependent on an annual subsidy, called the *situado*, sent from the Royal Treasury in New Spain. The amount depended upon the number of personnel assigned to the fort and the maintenance costs. The *situado* was frequently slow in arriving and in some years it did not arrive at all. As a result, the Spanish often resorted to illegal trade with the French in Mobile.[4]

Money was not the only problem. Storms and high tides continually ravaged the island settlement. In November of 1752 a hurricane howled out of the Gulf of Mexico and struck the island. When the skies cleared, only two buildings remained standing. Many inhabitants decided to move to the mainland where the small blockhouse, San Miguel, had been built a few miles east of the entrance to the bay (in present day Seville Square). Some of the civilians immediately sought the protection of this fort although the government offices continued to remain on the island for another month.[5]

By 1757 the entire population had moved to the San Miguel area. Threats of Indian attacks on the inadequately protected Spanish caused the new viceroy, Marques de las Amarillos, to conclude that a new

"A Perspective View of Pensacola," drawn by Dom Serres in 1743, is the only known illustration of the Island village. Nothing remains of this settlement. Pensacola Historical Society photo.

town and presidio should be built near the San Miguel blockhouse. The presidio was first called *San Miguel de las Amarillas*, but the name was changed in 1757. The new town was henceforth to be known as *Presidio San Miguel de Panzacola.*[6] By 1760 a church, a hospital, the government house, a storehouse, a bake oven, a barracks for troops and a barracks for the labor battalion had been built.[7]

Yet another hurricane pounded Pensacola in 1760, destroying the island town and causing great damage to the mainland settlement. When Great Britain acquired Pensacola in 1763, the Spanish were still in the process of rebuilding the town.

7   HIS MAJESTY'S LOYAL COLONY

In 1763 the Spanish soldiers and civilians once again boarded their ships and sailed away from Pensacola. Article XX of the Treaty of Ghent ending the Seven Years War stated: "his most Catholic Majesty cedes and guarantees in full right, to His Britannic Majesty, Florida, with Fort St. Augustine, and the Bay of Pensacola, as well as all that Spain possesses on the continent of North America to the east, or to the southeast of the River Mississippi."[1] The stately language of the treaty provided for an orderly transfer of the territory which the British divided into the provinces of East and West Florida. Pensacola was designated the capital of West Florida which extended from the Apalachicola River to the Mississippi River as far north as present day Vicksburg.

Lt. Colonel Augustin Prevost of the Third Royal American Regiment assumed command at Pensacola on August 6, 1763. He was distinctly unimpressed with what he found in the small village and sent a derogatory report to his superiors in London:

> The country from the insufferable laziness of the Spaniards remains still uncultivated, the woods are close to the village and a few haltry [paltry] gardens show the only improvements. The climate is not healthy, the soil around the village though sandy is able to produce vegetables; further back the country is good and capable of improvement — but years and a number of industrious settlers can only make a change on the face of the colony. Stock they have none, being entirely supplied from Mobile — game is plenty in the woods and the sea supplies quantities of fish of different sorts and kinds.[2]

Major William Forbes, commanding officer of the 35th Regiment of Foot, arrived in Pensacola in the fall. He, too, reported a dismal assessment of Pensacola.

> I arrived here with the 35th Regimt [sic.] the 30th of

gave birth to their son, Philip, during the Battle of Mobile. Durnford was released on parole and returned to England. He was subsequently sent to Tobago in the West Indies where he died from yellow fever in 1792. Pensacola Historical Society photo.

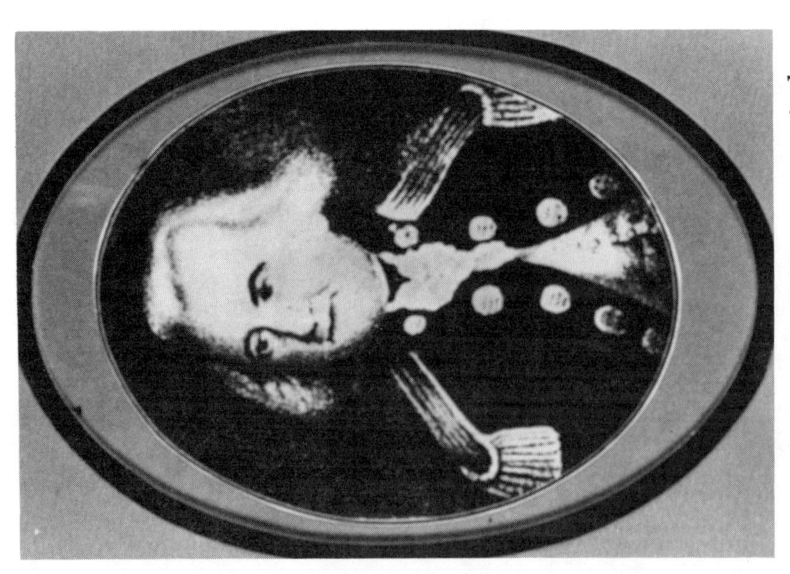

Elias Durnford, described as one of the most capable of British West Florida's civil and military officers, served as surveyor general, was a member of the town council and was in command of the troops at Mobile when that city fell to Gálvez. Family history indicates that Rebecca Durnford

November last. The place which is called the Fort consists of about half a mile of ground in circumference surrounded with a rotten stockade without a ditch, so defenceless that anyone can step in at pleasure, the Barracks of the Officers and Soldiers are nothing more than miserable bark hutts [*sic.*], without any sort of Fire places or windows, void of every necessary utencil [*sic.*].[3]

Perhaps the British did not know of the devastating hurricanes which had destroyed much of Spanish Pensacola. At any rate, with typical British efficiency they set out to improve conditions in Pensacola and eventually they established a thriving settlement by the bay. In one respect, the new colony of British West Florida followed the Spanish precedent. West Florida became a Crown Colony subsidized by the home government and continued to be a garrison town.

Civilian settlement was encouraged by a system of land grants from the crown. These land grants were obtained under the same quit-rent system that was used in other colonies. Even though both eligible soldiers and civilians obtained land through the system, the rents were often in arrears. Sparse settlement throughout the colony precluded enforcement of rent collection.[4] Most of the land grants were in the hinterlands between Pensacola and the Mississippi River.

Land ownership in the town of Pensacola was complicated by the fact that many of the departing Spaniards sold land to the incoming British. An international controversy surrounded these transactions. The British government did not recognize the sales; the Spanish government protested that their former owners were never fully compensated for the sales. Some of the great names of England were involved in the dispute. James Noble formed an investment company which included the Dukes of York and Cumberland, the Earl of Bute, Lord Mansfield and others. The company paid 100,000 pesos for land bought from the Yamassee Indians who had gone to Vera Cruz with the Spanish in 1763. The company's petition to keep the land was refused by the crown for lack of sufficient evidence.[5]

If James Noble was an example of the speculative British businessman, then Elias Durnford was an example of the dedicated British civil servant and colonizer. Durnford, who was both a military officer and a surveyor, was ordered by the new Council for West Florida to present a plan for the town. He carefully platted streets, lots with gardens, sites for the fort and barracks and locations for other

The first British Governor of West Florida, George Johnstone, acquired a reputation for gallantry in the Royal Navy and by 1762, when he was less than thirty-five years old, he had attained the rank of post captain. A caustic and controversial individual, Johnstone frequently argued with the military authorities and the Pensacola town council, causing unnecessary strife in the colony. After his recall in 1767, Johnstone served in Parliament and was regarded as an authority on American affairs. In 1778 he was appointed to the Carlisle Commission which attempted to conciliate the colonies. The Continental Congress refused to deal with either Johnstone or the commission. Author's photo. Cecil Johnson, "Pensacola in the British Period, Summary and Significance," *Florida Historical Quarterly*, 37, nos. 3 & 4 (Jan.-Apr. 1959), 266.

public buildings. The private lots measured 80 feet by 160 feet. Each of these lots was assigned a garden bordering on a small stream which flowed by the north end of the village. The aptly named Garden Street divided the two types of lots. The purchasers of the now void Spanish claims received the first choice of lots. Second choice was given to holders of government positions. The remaining lots were purchased by others who could meet the requirement that the property must be developed for future use. The streets were laid at right angles to each other and were of uniform width.[6] This basic plan can still be seen in the streets of the Seville Square Historic District.

The ambitious town plan did not bring scores of new settlers into Pensacola. The town was isolated from the rest of West Florida. Overland travel to Pensacola from other areas of West Florida was almost impossible. The long water route from the Mississippi River settlements passed by Spanish New Orleans and passage downriver was unpredictable. Pensacola was simply the seat of the government of the colony and primarily a garrison town.[7]

West Florida's government was typical of a British Royal Province or Crown Colony. The king appointed the governor, lieutenant-governor and members of the council. The council was the upper house of a bicameral legislature. The lower house, called the assembly, was elected by the inhabitants of the colony. A royally appointed chief justice presided over the judiciary. This civil establishment was entirely supported by an annual appropriation from Parliament. This subsidy represented a departure from normal crown colony finance but was necessary because of the frontier character of the new possession. While the subsidy freed the citizen from any tax burden, it also freed the governor from any dependence upon the elected assembly.[8]

West Florida's first governor, George Johnstone, arrived in Pensacola on October 21, 1764. He brought with him a reputation for con-

British cartographer George Gauld drew the first perspective view of the mainland in the 1760s. Photo from Special Collections, John C. Pace Library, University of West Florida.

troversy and quarreling; it was greatly enhanced by his stay in Pensacola. His continual bickering with the military establishment and the assembly overshadowed his valid contributions to the development of the colony. Johnstone tried to overcome at least two main obstacles to the growth of West Florida.

He immediately tackled the Indian problem. In order for the colony to develop, peace with the local tribes had to be ensured. Johnstone and the Superintendent for Indian Affairs, John Stuart, held meetings amid formal surroundings to impress the tribal chiefs. Trade agreements were signed with the Creek, Choctaw and Chickasaw Indian tribes. Both sides cheated on the provisions and the problem of Indian trade was never fully solved.[9]

Since trade was vital to the economy of the colony, Johnstone made attempts to overcome obstacles to transactions with the Spanish. Transportation of goods to West Florida in British vessels from Spanish lands was legal; it was illegal in Spanish vessels. In spite of protestations to the Board of Trade, Johnstone never succeeded in removing this obstacle.[10] Continuous quarreling with the military commanders over petty problems of command stained Johnstone's record as governor. The age-old conflict between civil and military establishments required tact and diplomacy along the frontier. A strong military garrison was essential due to the frontier nature of both the capital and the rest of the colony. The governor also wanted a strong civil government. The two became incompatible primarily due to Johnstone's bellicose attitude.

The constant bickering marked by numerous letters to and from the authorities in London could not be tolerated. Governor Johnstone was relieved of his duties in February, 1767.[11]

Lt. Governor Montfort Browne assumed the governorship when Johnstone departed. Browne had been involved in many of the quarrels of the previous administration. When the new governor, John Eliot, arrived in the spring of 1769, he found Browne under attack by the local populace who accused him of issuing false vouchers for expenditures charged to the contingency fund. The citizens expected Eliot to restore confidence in the government. But this was not to be. The new governor hanged himself on May 2.[12] Browne once again assumed the governorship. Since he regarded Elias Durnford as a friend, he asked the surveyor, who was returning to England on leave, to take an accounting of the affairs of the colony back to London. Much to Browne's surprise, Durnford returned with a commission for himself to replace

Commander of Spanish forces during the Siege of Pensacola, Bernardo de Gálvez, was young, energetic and a born leader. A native of Malaga, Spain, Gálvez joined the army as a young man. After service in Portugal, he joined his uncle's entourage in New Spain where he was second-in-command of expeditions against the Apaches. He returned to Spain for a brief time before arriving in Louisiana in 1776 as Colonel of the Regiment. When Spain declared war against Great Britain in 1779, he became Governor of Louisiana. He was popular and well regarded by colonists for his enlightened policies.

Gálvez achieved fame as a general. He quickly saw the opportunity to oust the British from the Mississippi and Gulf regions following the declaration of war. After taking British posts along the river, he captured Mobile. Then, he captured Pensacola in a sixty-one day siege ending in May 1781. For his heroic action during the Pensacola campaign he was made Count of Gálvez and granted a coat of arms by the King with the following citation: ". . . to perpetuate in your posterity the memory of the heroic action in which you, alone, forced your entry into said Bay, you may put as a Seal on your Coat of Arms the Brigantine Gálvez-town with the Motto: I ALONE . . ."

Gálvez died in Mexico City in 1786, the victim of an epidemic of unknown origins. Sandra Johnson "Born to Destiny: Bernardo de Gálvez" *Siege! Spain and Britain: Battle of Pensacola March 9-May 8, 1781* (Pensacola Historical Society, 1981). *Photo from Louisiana Arts and Science Center, Baton Rouge, Louisiana.*

Browne as acting governor. More quarrels and bickering, reminiscent of the Johnstone administration, erupted. The colony was in near chaos as far as the civil government was concerned.

Order was finally restored when a new governor, Peter Chester, arrived in 1770. Chester was an able administrator, but he also quarreled with the assembly over appropriations and privileges. Chester solved the problem by refusing to call more than one meeting of the assembly.[13]

Because of the dependency on London, isolation of the colony and failure of the legislature to meet, Pensacola and West Florida remained loyal to the Crown during the American Revolution. Chester prevented publication of an overture to the citizens of West Florida from the Continental Congress in 1774 urging them to join the American cause.[14] Since the region prospered during the decade of the 1770s, the colonists saw no reason to change the status quo.

The Americans ignored Pensacola. The Spanish did not. Spain soon seized an opportunity to reclaim Pensacola.

In 1777 a young, energetic nobleman, Bernardo de Gálvez, became the Spanish Governor of Louisiana. One of his first acts was to strengthen the military complement of his territory by recruiting and training a local militia. He sought Indian alliances and courted the Americans' favor by offering trade privileges and refuge in his province.

Spain entered the American Revolutionary War in 1779 as an ally of France; not of the Americans. Gálvez was well prepared to attack the British possessions of West Florida. He captured the settlements along the Mississippi River during the summer and early fall of 1779. After consolidating these positions, he was ready to turn east towards Mobile and Pensacola.

Defended by 300 troops under the command of Lieutenant Governor Elias Durnford, Mobile experienced a gentlemanly battle interrupted by parlays between Durnford and Gálvez. Durnford tried to stall the impending Spanish attack until reinforcements from Pensacola could reach Mobile. The fresh troops did not reach him before the Spanish breached the walls of the fort. Durnford surrendered Mobile in March 1780.[15]

Gálvez was now free to gather forces for an assault on the capital of British West Florida. He recruited reinforcements from Havana and amassed an armada of sixty-four ships to attack Pensacola.

Governor Chester and the military commander, General John

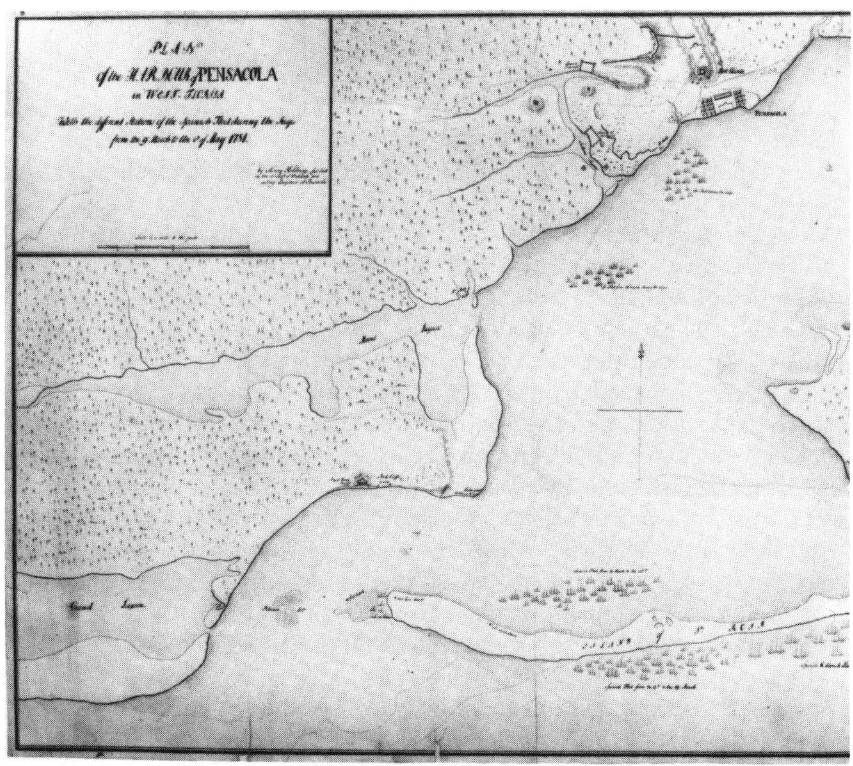

The "Plan of the Siege of Fort George and Works Adjacent at Pensacola in West Florida 1781" by Captain Lieutenant Henry Heldring of the Third Regiment of Waldeck traces the route taken by Bernardo de Gálvez from the Red Cliffs to the final siege of Fort George. Photo from William L. Clements Library, University of Michigan, Ann Arbor, Michigan.

Campbell, were, of course, aware of Gálvez' intentions. Campbell reinforced Fort George which had been built in 1778 on Gage Hill north of town. Campbell also had plans for a blockhouse at the western tip of Santa Rosa Island. The blockhouse was never built. Its purpose was to control the entrance to the bay in conjunction with the naval redoubt at Red Cliffs near old Fort San Carlos. Pensacola was defended by British regulars, reinforced by a regiment of German Waldecks and a contingent of American Loyalist troops. The entire force consisted of 1,200 men, but only 750 were fit for duty. The sickness rate was high and the men suffered from a variety of fevers, malaria, small pox and scurvy.[16]

On the morning of March 8, 1781, the invading Spanish fleet loomed off Santa Rosa Island. The next day troops landed on the island. After some disagreements with Captain José Calbo de Irazábal, the senior naval officer present, Gálvez, himself, led the Spanish ships into Pensacola Bay and supervised a landing near Barrancas.

Thirteen hundred troops had come with Gálvez. They were soon reinforced by 900 men from Mobile and 1,400 men from New Orleans.

Gálvez began an encircling movement, crossing bayous and streams until his troops were in a position to attack Fort George and its two redoubts. He was met with resistance along the march by British troops and their Indian allies. When he finally dug in to the west of Fort George, a siege situation began. The Spanish fired artillery pieces at the fort for several days and their fire was returned. On May 8, 1781, a lucky shot hit the powder magazine of Queen's Redoubt. The redoubt, which was designed to defend Fort George, was destroyed. General Campbell was obliged to surrender his command and the Spanish flag once again flew over Pensacola.[17]

The siege and conquest of Pensacola by Gálvez are a footnote to the history of the American Revolution. Yet, the fact that the Spanish general kept British attention focused on the province of West Florida for over a year contributed to the success of the Revolution. General Cornwallis could have used the Pensacola troops in his southeastern campaign which led to defeat at Yorktown.

8   SUNSET OF AN EMPIRE

In 1781 Pensacola was once again a Spanish town, stretching along the waterfront for about one mile and extending one quarter of a mile inland. Swamps bounded Pensacola on the north side and two streams which rose under Gage Hill provided natural east and west boundaries. It was still an isolated town. The nearest settlements were Mobile to the west and St. Marks to the east. Wilderness still existed to the north. Communication with the outside world was primarily dependent upon sea travel for only poorly marked trails inched through the piney woods.

Pensacola retained its British character. Town blocks were divided into twelve lots each although few of these boasted dwellings. All of the 200 houses were of wood construction with front porches. Most of the houses were one-story structures and many were surrounded by wooden fences. The principal government buildings, the governor's house, the barracks and several storehouses were located within a cypress-stake enclosure.[1]

The Spanish changed the old British street names to those that remain today. Palafox Street was named either for the Spanish General Palafox who was taken prisoner during the siege of Zaragoza or for the Bishop of Puebla. Zaragoza also became a street name. Other street names reflected the Golden Age of Spain: Baylen for the Spanish city where French forces surrendered; Alcaniz, another Spanish town where the French were defeated; Romana for a famous Spanish general; Barcelona and Seville were namesakes of old Spanish cities.[2]

Almost the entire British population left Pensacola with the change of flags. The new Spanish settlers came primarily from Spanish Louisiana, the Canary Islands and from the French Creole populations of other Caribbean islands.

At least one British subject joined the new arrivals. William Panton and his partners, most prominently John Leslie, had established a thriving business in St. Augustine. They received deer skins from the Indians in trade for guns, ammunition and other goods from England. Deerskin garments, particularly coats, were extremely popular in Europe. Panton, a canny Scot, realized that one of Pensacola's major

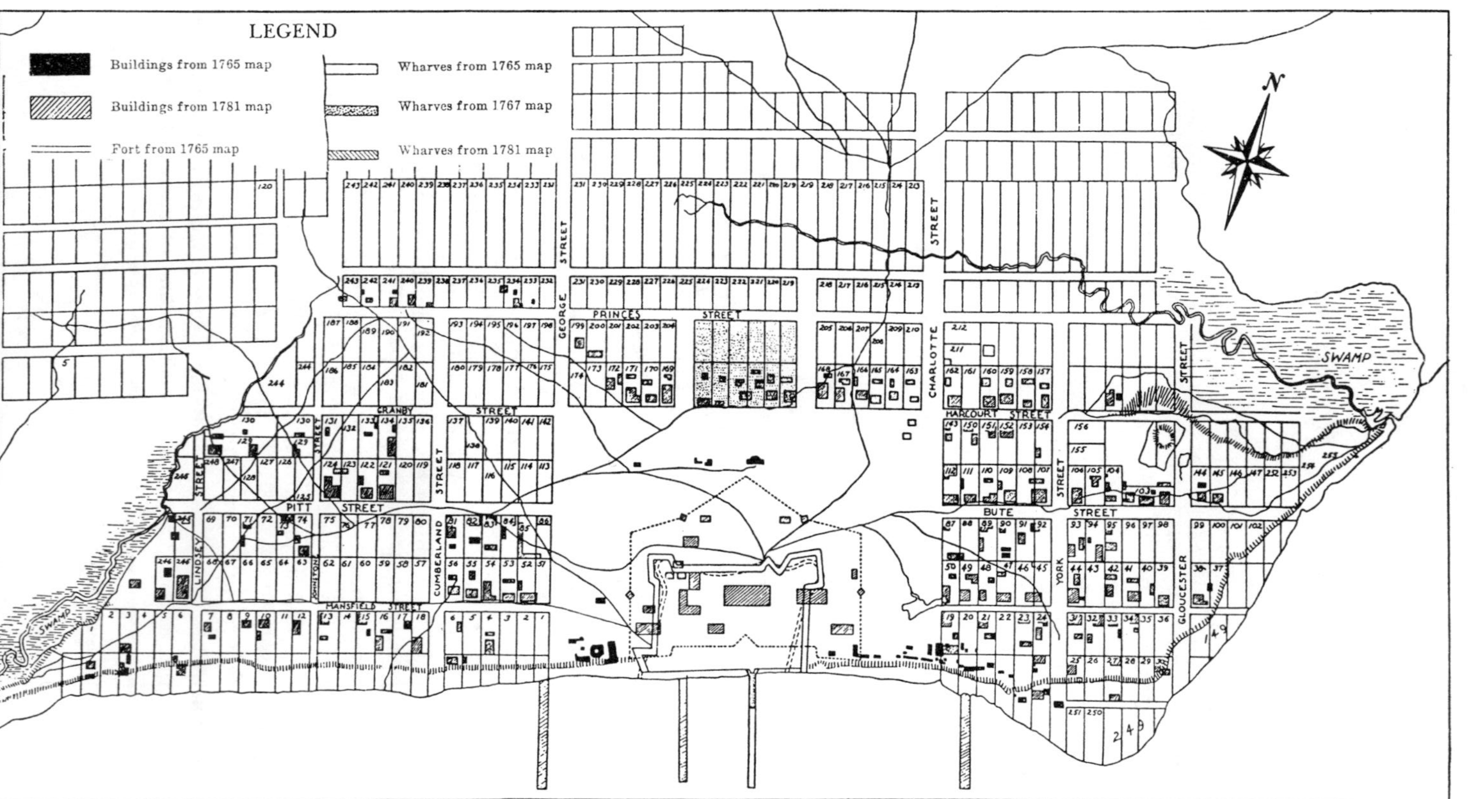

Town Plan of Pensacola under the British, 1766-1781. Clinton N. Howard, *The British Development of West Florida, 1763-1769* (Berkeley & Los Angeles: University of California Press, 1947), *folg. p. 42.*

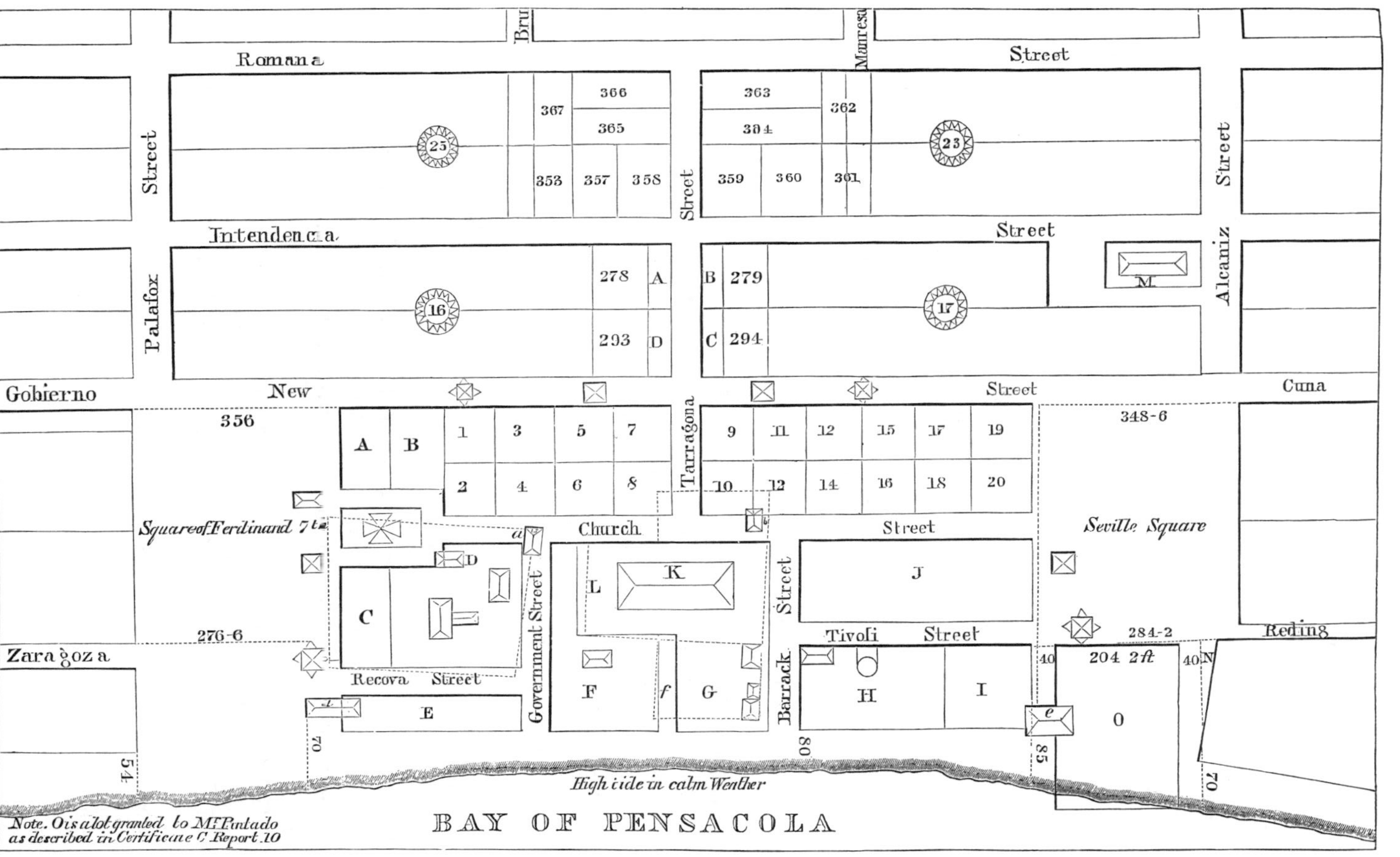

Town Plan of Pensacola under the Spaniards, ca. 1815-1821. American State Papers, Public Lands, 4:231.

drawbacks could be turned to his advantage.

The drawback was the geography of the area. The vast interior wilderness lay almost at Pensacola's doorstep. The great bay provided a fine natural harbor and the sea routes from the bay were Pensacola's only link with the outside world. Panton decided to corner the Indian trade market and to procure ships to transport goods to and from England.[3]

The success of the Panton enterprise was enhanced by a remarkable Creek Indian, Alexander McGillivray. McGillivray, the son of a Scottish trader and a Creek Indian woman, was educated in Charleston, South Carolina. He became the head man of the Wind Clan of the Creek Indians and he was also William Panton's friend.[4]

Panton, with McGillivray as a silent partner, built a profitable trading business based in Pensacola and San Marcos de Apalache (St. Marks). The Creeks provided Panton with skins in return for the goods they desired. Panton built a large trading post in Pensacola along the bayfront. He employed between seventy-five and eighty workmen and clerks to handle the shipments of skins and goods. A small fleet of ocean-going vessels plied between English ports and Pensacola. Smaller vessels served the coastal towns of St. Marks, Mobile and New Orleans. Panton became the wealthiest man in Pensacola; after his death, the company assets were valued at 396,800 pesos.[5]

The Creeks came to Panton's Pensacola headquarters and traded deerskins valued at fourteen pence sterling per pound for salt at nine shillings per bushel. Panton transported the salt to Pensacola from the company salt pans in the Bahamas in company ships at an average cost of three pence per bushel. The profits from the salt trade alone have been estimated at 500 per cent.[6]

In addition to the Indian trade, Panton furnished the Pensacola garrison with meat and other provisions which he obtained cheaply from the Indians in repayment for old debts. Panton also acted as banker for the inhabitants of Pensacola and advanced goods on credit to the Spanish garrison.[7]

Alexander McGillivray played a significant role in the early success of Panton, Leslie and Company. He convinced the Indians to trade almost exclusively with Panton. McGillivray's motives were pragmatic: he received a portion of the company profits until 1788 and he was interested in the survival of the Creek Nation which was threatened by the Americans on the eastern seaboard. It was obvious that the Americans would eventually settle in lands belonging to the Creeks.

As a hedge against American encroachment on his lands, McGillivray entered into a secret treaty with the United States in 1790. He knew that the ultimate disposition of the Creek Nation depended upon the disputed boundary in North America between the Spanish and American territories. McGillivray promised emergency trade with the Americans in the event that the existing trade routes with Great Britain were closed. In return for this promise, the Americans made McGillivray a brigadier general with an annual stipend of $1,200. He continued his liaison with Panton.[8]

The friendship ended with McGillivray's death in 1793.[9] Two years later the Treaty of 1795 (Pinckney's Treaty) established the dividing line between the United States and Spanish West Florida at the 31st parallel (latitude 31° north). This action placed most of Panton, Leslie's Indian customers in United States territory. At this point the company began to decline.[10]

Alexander McGillivray, son of Scot trader Lachlan McGillivray and a Creek Indian woman named Sehoy, chose to live among Creeks where mixed blood was not a handicap as in the Anglo-American communities. After early training from his mother he attended school in Charleston at fourteen, studying Greek, Latin and English history until his studies were interrupted by the American Revolution. Lachlan McGillivray, a loyalist on the American's proscribed list, returned to Scotland. Alexander returned to the Creeks who gave him the rank of a lesser chief of the Wind Clan. The British commissioned him a colonel to maintain his loyalty which they probably could have had anyway since McGillivray both hated and feared the encroaching Americns. His goal was to keep Creek lands for Creeks. Described as tall and slender, with a gravity of bearing and immobility of expression, McGillivray's piercing eyes glared from below an abnormally broad and high forehead. McGillivray frequently dressed as a white man and his house was presided over by an Indian squaw. His friendship with William Panton was a basis for the vast Panton-Leslie trading empire. John Walton Caughey, McGillivray of the Creeks (Norman: University of Oklahoma Press, 1938). Pensacola Historical Society photo.

William Panton died at sea in 1801. The old Panton-Leslie firm became known as John Forbes & Co. in 1804. In 1807 Forbes retired and control of the company passed to the Innerarity family.[11]

In spite of the vast scope and wealth of the Panton business, Pensacola remained essentially a garrison town. Spain continued to send an annual *situado* to support the population. Business revolved around the disbursement of these monies as well as the Panton-Leslie trade. Few Pensacolians were engaged in the direct production of goods. Most of the town's businesses concerned trade and services provided to the garrison.

Life in Pensacola was relaxed and informal. In contrast to the first Spanish occupation, most of the food now came from local vegetable gardens and from fishing. Two butchers, one for the garrison and one for the civilians, handled beef bought from the Indians.

In 1810 there were no public buildings of any importance. One two-story building, formerly the residence of the British governor, was used as a barracks. Church services were held in a warehouse. Two small industries were harbingers of greater things to come. Governor Vicente Folch owned two small sawmills about sixteen miles from the town on a branch of the Escambia River. A brickyard located on the opposite side of the bay from the town produced paving tiles and bricks. American homespun cotton was available in local stores and Negro women peddled goods from baskets. There were no printers, potters, tinsmiths, coppersmiths, watchmakers, hatters or saddlers. There were two tailors.[12]

The town, however, was growing. In 1814 the garden lots which Durnford had designed to go with the town lots were subdivided and sold at auction. Some streets were blocked by a helter-skelter pattern of home construction. The large Plaza was partially sub-divided leaving two public squares called Ferdinand VII and Seville. Each square measured 500 by 300 feet.[13]

Social life revolved around the governor's wife. The ladies followed the French fashion scene, wearing dresses without trains and with short sleeves. Several taverns and billiard rooms offered acceptable entertainment for the men of the town. Religious life centered around the Catholic Church, the state religion of Spain.[14]

The population continued to increase; the town was becoming more cosmopolitan as more and more Americans joined the Spanish settlers.[15] Although it was still a predominantly Spanish town, a change was on the horizon.

9 "Scalp For Scalp"

The Americanization of Pensacola resulted from the ambitions of one man: Andrew Jackson. Andrew Jackson hated the British; he also hated Indians. Great Britain had not forgotten her interests in West Florida and openly supported the Spanish in the region. The Creek Indians resented American settlers on their lands. Alarmed by British and Indian intrigue in the province, Jackson viewed West Florida as territory which should be part of the United States.

Spanish territory in North America had shrunk drastically by 1814. The Louisiana Purchase of 1803 resulted from a complicated series of negotiations between Spain and France and then between France and the United States. It deprived Spain of a large part of her territory along the Mississippi River. The articles of the Purchase treaty left the boundaries of Spanish West Florida vague. The United States, without any real justification, claimed all the land west of the Perdido River as part of the Louisiana Purchase, but Spain continued to occupy the area between Pensacola and New Orleans.[1]

The Spanish maintained a tenuous hold on the disputed territory until 1810 when the United States gained possession of the area between the Pearl and Mississippi Rivers. In the spring of 1813 American troops under the command of General James Wilkinson marched unopposed into Mobile and completed the occupation of the land west of the Perdido River. During the summer the Red Stick faction of the Creek Indians went on the warpath and massacred 500 people who had taken shelter at Fort Mims, north of Mobile.[2]

Word of the massacre spread to Nashville, Tennessee, where Andrew Jackson was recuperating from wounds received during a gun fight with the Benton brothers. The two Bentons had slurred the name of Jackson's wife, Rachel, who falsely believed that her first husband had obtained a divorce before she married Jackson. Ignoring his injuries, Jackson led his Tennessee forces against the Red Sticks and defeated them at Horseshoe Bend on March 27, 1814. Many Indian survivors fled to Pensacola.[3]

A British squadron had dropped anchor in Pensacola Bay. Following the American occupation of Mobile, Spanish Governor Gonzales

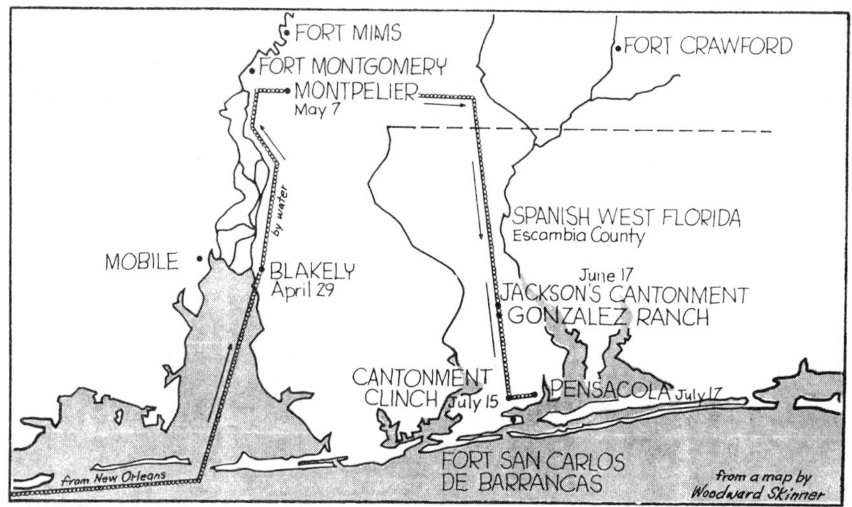

Route followed by Governor Andrew Jackson to Pensacola in the summer of 1821 showing place names enroute. Map courtesy of Woodward B. Skinner.

Manrique allowed the officers and soldiers aboard the British ships to occupy Fort San Miguel and Fort Barrancas. Jackson now marched on Pensacola and sent a message to the Spanish Governor demanding an explanation of the British presence as well as the surrender of three hostile Indian Chiefs who had sought refuge in the town. When Gonzales Manrique refused either to surrender the chiefs or to acknowledge the British presence, Jackson fired back using an updated Biblical warning, "An Eye for an Eye, Tooth for Tooth and Scalp for Scalp," and attacked Pensacola. Poor Gonzales Manrique was reportedly rushing around the town with a white flag of surrender trying to find Jackson. Actually, the governor was nearly blind. At any rate, the hated British were expelled from Pensacola and Jackson returned the town to Spanish rule.[4]

The British now began to aid the Indians of West Florida in the Apalachicola River area. In 1818 Jackson once again invaded Florida. This time he captured Fort St. Marks near the mouth of the river. He also executed a former British officer and a British merchant who had been aiding the Indians and the escaped slaves.[5]

Jackson now marched toward Pensacola; he again took the city and also Fort Barrancas. He shipped the prisoners to Cuba and installed an American military governor: Colonel William King. Jackson then returned to Tennessee, leaving the negotiations over sovereignty to the diplomats.[6]

The Spanish government immediately protested to the United States government. Authorities in Washington agreed that Jackson had acted in a high-handed, independent manner and ordered the return of both the town and the forts to Spain. It was now quite obvious, however, that the Americans could take West Florida by force of arms at any time. Realizing this fact, the Spanish entered into negotiations with the United States concerning the Floridas. After protracted discussions the Adams-Onís treaty was finally signed on February 22, 1819 and quickly ratified by the United States Senate. The Spanish government delayed final action indulging in their favorite pastime — procrastination. Finally, Spain signed the treaty and Pensacola officially became an American city on February 22, 1820, but five months passed before American rule was established.[7]

Andrew Jackson was the obvious choice for the first governor of Florida. He received his commission from President James Monroe on March 12, 1821 with orders to receive the ceded territory for the United States and to establish a territorial government in Florida. President Monroe also made ten other appointments: three judges, two district attorneys, two secretaries and three collectors. Left with little appointive power of his own, Jackson resolved to resign as governor as soon as the territory became self-governing.[8]

Transfer of Pensacola and West Florida to the United States met with typical Spanish procrastination. Although the land records for East Florida were seized by the United States troops, the delivery of the West Florida records were delayed by Spanish authorities. For five weeks, Jackson, along with his wife and two adopted sons, waited at Blakeley, Alabama for a surrender authorization to arrive from Cuba. During that time, he entered into a cordial correspondence with Governor José Callava of Pensacola and Jackson mistakenly got the impression that there would be no trouble from Callava.

Andrew Jackson spent much of his adult life defending his wife's honor. When he married Mrs. Rachel Donelson Robards, she erroneously believed her first husband had obtained a divorce in Virginia. The divorce was actually granted two years later. Scandalous stories, circulating about Rachel never failed to provoke Jackson's wrath. An implied slur on Rachel's honor sparked Jackson's duel with the Benton brothers. Rachel Jackson died during the presidential campaign of 1828. "Old Hickory," as Jackson had come to be known, took the oath of office without her at his side.
Pensacola Historical Society photo.

Frontiersman, soldier, statesman — Andrew Jackson was all three. Tall and slender, he typified the United States westerner of the early nineteenth century. Strong-willed, hot-tempered and impatient of op- position, he made warm friends and bitter enemies. As a soldier, he was accustomed to winning; as a statesman, he assumed a mantle of leadership. All of these qualities were seen during his Florida years. When the War of 1812 began, Jackson volunteered the Tennessee militia and led it to victory over Creek Indians at Horseshoe Bend. In recognition of his victory, Jackson was commissioned a major general in the United States Army and ordered to protect the southwestern border. He captured Spanish-held Pensacola and planned further Florida operations when he was ordered to defend the city of New Orleans. His major victory of the Battle of New Orleans in 1815 brought national attention. His subsequent forays into Florida made his name known throughout the country. Pensacola Historical Society photo.

Finally Jackson grew tired of the waiting. He entered Florida accompanied by the United States Fourth Infantry Regiment. Jackson stopped at Gonzalia, the home of Don Manuel Gonzalez, fifteen miles north of the city. From Gonzalia Jackson issued an invitation to Governor Callava to meet and discuss the delay. The proud Callava had expected Jackson to make the first call and to bring his credentials with him. Equally proud, Jackson stated: "I would sink this place and him with it before I would visit him."[9]

While this exchange of notes was in progress, the transfer papers finally arrived from Havana. Jackson sent Rachel and the two boys on to Pensacola. He would not enter the city until the date of transfer. Callava continued to delay until Jackson threatened to take Pensacola by force. Callava's resistance immediately collapsed and he agreed to surrender West Florida at 10 a.m. on July 17. Swallowing his pride, Jackson entered the city on that date and called on Callava. The official transfer of Pensacola to the United States took place in Government House. Following the signing of the papers, the old and the new governors emerged and marched through two columns of troops, Spanish on one side and American on the other, to Plaza Ferdinand VII. The Spanish flag was lowered and the United States flag was raised; the United States sloop *Hornet* fired a 21 gun salute; and *The Star Spangled Banner* was played for the first time in Pensacola. The Spanish troops then marched to the pier for embarkation. The era of American government had begun.[10]

10   "Such A Mixed Multitude"

Mrs. Andrew Jackson certainly did not like Pensacola. In 1821 she wrote:

> The inhabitants all speak Spanish and French. Some speak four or five languages. Such a mixed multitude, you, nor any of us, ever had an idea of . . . Fewer white people by far than any other . . . Seamen strolled with knives in their belts and coins burning their pockets; absurd little Spanish soldiers; yellow women with well-turned limbs and insinuating glances; Jamaica blacks bearing prodigious burdens on their heads; a fish peddler filling the street with incomprehensible cries; a Seminole Indian with a set expression of unfriendliness; a grandee in his carriage. And must I say the worst people here are the cast-off Americans.[1]

As soon as Pensacola officially became an American town, Andrew and Rachel Jackson began to change the city from an easy-going Spanish town to a more structured American community. Rachel Jackson was horrified by the lack of morals and loose manners of the populace. She seemed particularly upset by the non-observance of the Sabbath. Within a week Andrew Jackson changed the ways of Pensacola and the Sabbath was observed on the following Sunday.[2]

Jackson's powers as Governor of Florida were unique and absolute. His commission granted him "all the powers and authorities heretofore exercised by the Governor and Captain-General and Intendant of Cuba, and by the Governors of East and West Florida."[3] Within a week after becoming governor, Jackson issued five major ordinances. He authorized the mayor and city council of Pensacola to make whatever regulations they deemed proper regarding the Christian Sabbath. Following Rachel's wishes, all theaters and gambling houses were closed on Sunday, a remarkable departure from Spanish rule. Jackson divided Florida into two counties, Escambia and St. Johns. He established Courts of Justice; set up regulations for judicial procedures; and set up a list of fees for civil services.[4]

Don Francisco Moreno can be called "The Father of Pensacola," for he married three times and had a total of twenty-seven children. His family's history spanned a large period of Pensacola's history. One hundred and seventy-one years passed between the birth of Francisco Moreno in 1792 and the death of his youngest child in 1963.

Born in Pensacola, Francisco Moreno was the son of Don Fernando Moreno. Francisco married Josepha López in 1814 and three children were born to this union. Their oldest daughter, Angela, married Stephen R. Mallory, who became Confederate Secretary of the Navy. Following Josepha's death, Moreno married her sister, Margarita Eleutaria López. Twelve children came from this union. After Margarita died, Moreno married Mentoria Gonzalez and fathered twelve more children.

When the United States acquired Florida, Moreno elected to remain in Pensacola though he never gave up his Spanish citizenship. Supposedly, he kept a trunk filled with money which he lent to needy persons on signature alone. Even though he was the Spanish consul in Pensacola, he was an ardent supporter of the Confederacy during the Civil War. When most Pensacolians fled the city, Moreno remained. Five of his sons fought for the Confederacy: one, Celestino, was killed during the skirmish in Columbia, Tennessee in 1861; another son, Francisco, wounded at Shiloh, died at Louisville on May 4, 1862. Don Francisco Moreno died in 1882. Pensacola Historical Society photo.

Jackson appointed Henry M. Brackenridge *alcalde* with orders to investigate the Spanish political system which was used in Pensacola. The *alcalde* was second only to the governor in importance. He exercised the duties of mayor, chief of police, sheriff, superintendent and inspector of prisons, and notary public. Brackenridge assumed all these duties.[5]

In an effort to Americanize Pensacola's population, Jackson registered all Spanish and other aliens. If their names remained on the registration rolls for twelve months, Jackson promised to consider them citizens of the United States. The United States Congress later annulled this act, stating that only Congress could exercise such power. Some residents of Pensacola never gave up their Spanish citizenship even though they remained in the city and occupied high positions in the new society.[6]

Many other Spanish citizens chose to leave the thriving little town of 2,000 people. Americans began arriving in greater numbers, causing a land boom. Prosperity increased with the arrival of Alabama and Mississippi cotton for export. The port began to hum with activity. In one week of 1824, 7,474 bales of cotton were exported from Pensacola to New Orleans. Lumber also began to be a prime industry, although in the early 1820s exports were small as compared to the post-Civil War boom years.[7]

The burgeoning commercial activity was inhibited by inadequate communication with the interior to the north. Wagon trains transported from the fields, a slow laborious journey. No navigable river connected the harbor with these regions. Southerly flowing rivers were the basic means of transportation to the other great ports on the Gulf of Mexico. The obvious answer to the northern communication problem was a railroad. Agitation for a railroad line to the north began almost immediately, but nothing came of these demands for fifteen years. The town prospered because it was the seat of the government of Florida.[8]

Andrew Jackson had set the government in motion. Yet, in his view, it was controlled by Washington. Jackson hoped to have the power to appoint his friends and political allies to high offices. He was not able to do this as many of the positions were appointed by President Monroe with little regard for Jackson's recommendations. Most administration was handled at the local level and Jackson found himself with little to do. Rachel wrote her brother in August 1821 that Jackson was anxious to return home to Tennessee. In November Jackson notified the President that the job of organizing an American government in Florida was completed. Old Hickory returned to the Hermitage in November 1821; his brief tenure as provisional governor of the Floridas was over.[9]

Pensacola was still the seat of the Territorial government and was the setting for the first session of the Legislative Council in 1822. James Bronaugh, an army surgeon and Jackson's personal physician, presided over the first meeting of the thirteen-man Council. A contest immediately developed between Dr. Bronaugh and Richard Keith Call over the post of delegate to the United States Congress. Each side was lining up supporters when a dreaded yellow fever epidemic erupted in Pensacola. The Council adjourned to the Gull Point residence of Don Juan de la Rua. Dr. Bronaugh contracted the disease and died along with approximately 236 others in the Pensacola area. The Council finally named Joseph M. Hernandez of St. Augustine the delegate to the United States Congress with a provision that a popular election would be held to fill the post in 1823.[10]

Andrew Jackson, shocked by the death of Dr. Bronaugh, wrote to his secretary, George Walton: "Pensacola is a healthy place with a proper police, and the present catastrophe is no evidence to my mind of the contrary. I have the prosperity of the Floridas much at heart, and its late dreadful visitation has filled my heart with woe."[11] Ironically, as one of his first acts as Governor, Jackson had issued a Public Health Ordinance which created a Board of Health consisting of the Mayor, the Aldermen and a Resident Physician. Dr. James Bronaugh had been appointed by Jackson to fill the latter post.[12]

Although the Legislative Council had agreed to alternate annual meetings between Pensacola and St. Augustine, it soon became apparent that travel between the two cities was difficult at best. A spot half way between the two places was chosen as the capital of the Territory of Florida and the third session of the Territorial Legislature met in a log cabin in a settlement that would become known as Tallahassee. No longer would Pensacola be the focal point of the government of Florida.[13]

Just as the government officials were leaving for the new capital of Tallahassee, a new era began in the old port city of Pensacola. In the colonial years Spain and Great Britain had fortified the harbor. The government of the United States decided to follow their examples in 1825. Commodore Lewis Warrington, Captain William Bainbridge and Captain James Biddle were commissioned by the Secretary of the Navy "to proceed to Pensacola and select a site for a naval establishment."[14] Their report cited the reasons for the choice of the old Tartar Point site for the naval base:

Between 1829 and 1835, George Washington Sully painted a series of watercolors of Pensacola and other small communities of northwest Florida, including a Pensacola residence reflecting the architectural style of the 1820s. Sully's father, a cotton merchant, moved his family to the new Florida Territory in the 1820s. George Washington Sully was for a brief time an employ of William H. Chase. Photo from Special Collections, John C. Pace Library, University of West Florida.

The Bay of Pensacola is extensive and capacious, easy of access from the sea, and affording secure anchorage for any number of vessels of the largest class. The depth of water on the bar . . . we believe, will always be (twenty-one feet). The ordinary tides do not rise more than three feet; but these tides run with considerable rapidity; thus affording facilities to vessels working in or out of the harbor against an unfavorable wind.

The position we have selected, as in our judgment combining the greatest advantages for a navy yard, is in the vicinity of the Barrancas, and to the northward and eastward of Tartar Point.

Here we found the necessary depth of water nearest the

shore; an important consideration in respect to the expense to be incurred in carrying out the wharves required for naval purposes. Here too the works erected for the defense of the navy yard, would give additional security to the harbor, while its vicinity to the Barrancas would admit of assistance to it in case of need, from the troops stationed there. Here, we are susceptible of complete defense, at a less expense than elsewhere within the bay. The position is wholly protected, by Tartar Point, against the swell of the sea, which strong southerly winds set over the bar.

Its healthiness is not surpassed by any other part of the bay, and fresh water is there abundant, and of a wholesome quality. Other positions, in other parts of the bay, have engaged our attention; but upon mature consideration, we are unanimously of the opinion that the position that we have designated is the most eligible under all circumstances, and combines the greatest advantages.[15]

Commodore Lewis Warrington became the first Commandant of the Pensacola Navy Yard on 20 April 1826. Construction of the yard had already begun although progress was slow due to shortages of materials and skilled local labor. Since Pensacola itself was some ten miles from the new yard, Commodore Warrington had the villages of Warrington and Woolsey laid out to the west and north of the yard on land owned by the government. The civilian workers were allowed to lease lots and to build on them.[16] To overcome the labor shortage, skilled workers from the north were recruited and Pensacola experienced its first wave of immigration associated with the navy.

The establishment of the Naval Live Oaks Reservation resulted from the navy's need for the live oak tree in ship building. In response to a Congressional Resolution, introduced by Florida Delegate Joseph M. White, Secretary of the Navy Samuel L. Southard declared it was his duty to "obtain, preserve and increase" live oak trees and recommended the "establishment of reservations in Florida and Louisiana for its [the live oak's] protection and cultivation."[17] Henry M. Brackenridge owned 1,360 acres in the center of government land on Santa Rosa Peninsula. In 1827 he sold 340 acres to the U. S. Navy for $2,200 and he also became the first superintendent of the Naval Live Oak Reservation in 1828.[18]

Naval officers enlivened Pensacola society and frequently

Old Christ Church in Seville Square was built in 1832 to serve Episcopalians, Methodists and Presbyterians of Pensacola. It remained an Episcopal Church after the other two congregations built their own churches. Designed in the Christopher Wren tradition, the church is the oldest still-standing church building in Florida. In 1903, the congregation moved to the new Christ Church on Wright Street. Subsequently used as a church by the parishoners of Saint Cyprian's Episcopal Church, the building later housed the city library and, since 1960 has been the Pensacola Historical Museum. Pensacola Historical Society photo.

cooperated with local officials in celebrations such as one for Fourth of July activities and a George Washington Birthday Ball.[19] Pensacola and the U. S. Navy had begun a long and profitable relationship.

The U. S. Army soon joined the navy on active duty in Pensacola. In order to protect the fledgeling navy yard, Congress authorized the building of three forts around the harbor. Once again, the sites originally chosen by Spain and Great Britain for fortifications were selected by the United States. In the 1830s construction began on Fort Pickens at the western tip of Santa Rosa Island, Fort McRee on Foster's Island and Fort Barrancas above and behind the old Spanish water battery, San Antonio. Forts Pickens and McRee were designed to protect water approaches to Pensacola; Fort Barrancas protected both the Navy Yard on the east and the land approaches on the north and west. The Barrancas Redoubt was erected approximately three fourths of a mile to the rear of Fort Barrancas as additional protection from a land attack on either Fort Barrancas or the Navy Yard. Captain William H. Chase of the U. S. Army Corps of Engineers was appointed to supervise the construction of the forts.[20]

Work on the forts was slow. The necessary bricks were shipped from Mobile until Captain Chase urged local businessmen to establish brick kilns using the high quality local clay deposits. Pensacola soon had a new industry, one of many which were to come as a direct result of the military presence in the area. Local labor was also scarce and contract slave labor was frequently used in the construction of the forts. Chase completed Fort Pickens by 1834 and began work on Fort McRee. Fort Barrancas was begun in 1839 and was virtually complete by 1844.[21]

Chase not only supervised the building of Pensacola's forts; he also was involved in civilian enterprises designed to promote the growth of Pensacola. He and several other men formed various companies to promote the building of a railroad from Pensacola north to Columbus, Georgia and to create a "New Town" east of Pensacola which would be on the rail line. Backed by the Bank of Pensacola, they laid out the area then known as the "New City" into lots and offered them for sale. Many lots were bought with a small down payment and three- or four-year mortgages. Construction began on the Florida, Alabama and Georgia Railroad. All of this activity came to a halt when the Bank of Pensacola failed as a result of the national Panic of 1837. The projects were resurrected in the 1850s. Construction of another rail line, the Alabama and Florida, was projected to Montgomery and completed to Pollard, Alabama, just prior to the Civil War. Pensacola finally had a

Captain William Henry Chase of the U. S. Army Corps of Engineers supervised the construction of Pensacola Harbor forts. When he arrived in the city in 1829, the West Point graduate had over a decade of engineering and construction experience. He emerged as one of Pensacola's leading businessmen and entrepreneurs. Since the forts and the navy yard required bricks and more bricks, Chase promoted Pensacola's brick manufacturing industry. He also became a landowner, joining others in forming a corporation to develop the "New City of Pensacola" east of the existing city limits. Chase, president of the board of Directors of the Alabama, Florida and Georgia Railroad, planned to construct a rail line from Alabama to a junction near the "New City." Although the plans collapsed during the Panic of 1837, they were revived in the 1850s with Chase still a leading figure in efforts to build rail connections north. He resigned from the army in 1856 and accepted the presidency of the Alabama and Florida Railroad. When the Civil War erupted, Chase, a native of Massachusetts, elected to support his adopted state, Florida. He commanded Confederate troops in the Pensacola area. Ernest F. Dibble, "William H. Chase: Fort and Prosperity Builder" *Antebellum Pensacola and the Military Presence* (Pensacola: Pensacola-Escambia Development Commission, 1974). T. T. Wentworth Collection photo.

An Aerial View of Fort Pickens. Battery Pensacola, constructed in 1898-99 is in the center of the fort. Pensacola Historical Society photo.

direct rail link with the north. The rails were destroyed during the war, but after Appomattox, the Montgomery line linked Pensacola with the northern interior.[22]

During the 1820s and 1830s the Territory of Florida was growing. The time was at hand for the Territory to apply for statehood. The U. S. Congress delayed action on Florida's petition because sectionalism was dividing the people. First, the location of the capital was tied with the inter-city rivalry between Pensacola and St. Augustine. This issue was resolved when Tallahassee was chosen to be the capital of Florida. A question arose as to whether the territory should enter the Union as one or two states. West Florida was closely tied to Alabama in both an economic and a geographical sense. Alabama campaigned for the annexation of the area around Pensacola and there were many Pensacolians who supported this idea. In the end, though, the entire area of the Territory of Florida joined the Union as one state in 1845.[23]

11 "THOSE ARCADIAN DAYS"

Pensacola slipped into a backwater role during the first few years following Florida's admission to the Union. Much of the city's social and economic life centered around the military presence. It might be said that the sobriquet "Pensacola, the Mother-in-law of the Navy" began during these years. One young naval officer, John McIntosh Kell, wrote in his autobiography:

> Pensacola in those days was the paradise of midshipmen. They, with their seniors, the lieutenants, gave themselves up to the gaities of this seaport town. It was always noted for the pretty girls that had their homes there, and of course they were always "belles" when the Gulf Squadron was at its rendezvous. Like the Norfolk [Virginia] girls they were very full of "sea knowledge." My friend, John N. Maffitt, in a charming little story of his, makes an old veteran officer say to a middy: "Mr. Forbes, a leopard cannot change its spots, neither can a Norfolk girl be otherwise than beautiful and d---d dangerous. At school their first class reader is 'Dorsey Lever.' Every Sunday they study the 'Navy Register,' and when standing on the 'Bridge of Sighs' with 'spoony' midshipmen by their sides they become instructors of astronomy, nautical romance and the abstruse science of knotting and splicing." Well, her Pensacola sisters can equal the Norfolk girl, and "sighing sailors, beautiful senoritas, scowling rivals and love-sick middies" filled the tropical air of that old town in my young days, and "music, moonlight, love, and flowers" were the living inspiration![1]

Both the Army and the Navy spurred the development of some local industries: notably the brick industry. Millions of bricks were needed for fort construction and local brickmakers satisfied this need. When the forts were completed, the brickmakers exported their product, principally to New Orleans. Contracts were also obtained for bricks for other fortifications. In 1853 a Pensacola brickmaker, probably H.

Palafox Street in 1860. This is one of the earliest known photographs of a Pensacola scene. T. T. Wentworth Collection photo.

F. Ingraham, supplied bricks for the construction of Fort Jefferson in the Dry Tortugas.[2] The most prominent brickmaking firm, Bacon and Abercrombie, produced eight million bricks in 1860. This firm employed 102 male and female employees during that year. The female workers were probably cooks.[3]

During these years, the lumber industry also emerged from the piney woods surrounding Pensacola. There had been small mills in the area since the British period, but technological advances — the use of the circular saw and the development of steam mills — expanded lumber operations. By 1860 local mills produced 54,913,000 feet of sawed lumber.[4] But, it was after the Civil War that the lumber industry really began to boom.

Pensacola's growth slowed and the population fluctuated during the antebellum years. One reason for the shifting population was the dreaded yellow fever. "There is no record of the number of cases and deaths from yellow fever in Pensacola during the 1840s. Nonetheless, its presence was probably a major factor contributing to Escambia County's lack of substantial growth."[5]

The worst of the 1850s epidemics occurred in 1853 when almost

PATGO

One form of amusement for Pensacolians in the 1820s was the great game of patgo. George A. McCall, a young Army officer stationed in Pensacola in 1821, described the game in a letter to his sister:

"A grand Patgo! . . . what is a Patgo, great or small? . . . It is an entertainment resembling in some measure the old Scottish "Popinjay shooting." The preliminaries are conducted in this way: a few days before the entertainment is to take place, the Host, having procured the figure of a fine chicken cock, of large size, fashioned out of a tough knotty block of wood, through which passes vertically an iron rod, whereupon the figure lightly whirls about like a weathercock. He sends this emblem of the gallant bird, mounted upon a staff, by a gayly dressed servant to the houses of the invited fair ones; and each lady presenting a bunch of ribbons or a feather for his toilet, soon his varied honors floating from his sides clothe him with a plumage of the brightest dyes.

On the day appointed for the fete, the Patgo or Game Bird is mounted on a high flag staff, and the gentlemen who are to contend for prizes, are assembled with their lady-loves under a spacious arbor erected for the occasion. This is at a distance of about sixty yards from the mark, at which the gallants are to try their skill with their rifles. Whenever a ribbon is cut down, the fortunate marksman brings it in to the bower, where it is acknowledged as her offering by the lady who had placed it on the bird; the gentleman thereupon claims her as his partner for the first dance to succeed the final destruction of the Patgo; he is likewise entitled to wear the trophy of his skill at his button-hole during the day." Drawing by Dianne Dusevitch.

every family in Pensacola suffered the loss of a member due to yellow jack. No one knew the cause of the disease; only that it was prevalent during the hot months near the seacoast and in marshy soils. "It was a disease of the towns and removal to the woods often protected people . . ."[6] Only 1,200 people remained in the city during the height of the epidemic and about 260 of those died of the fever.[7]

Despite such setbacks, Pensacola grew. In 1857 the railroad finally reached Pollard, Alabama and William H. Chase revived his dreams of a New City. Others, notably Senator Stephen R. Mallory, promoted Pensacola's shipbuilding for the U. S. Navy. As a result of his and other efforts, two ships were built at the navy yard between 1857 and 1859: the *USS Seminole* and the *USS Pensacola*. The *Seminole* was completely built in Pensacola, but the *Pensacola* was completed at the Navy Yard in Washington, D. C.[8]

The story of Pensacola during these years was best told by the son of Senator and Confederate Secretary of the Navy Stephen R. Mallory. In an article written for *The Pensacola Journal: Special Panama Canal Edition*, 1905-6, Stephen R. Mallory the younger reminisced:

> Of the period between 1830 and 1860, the history of Pensacola is practically a blank to all but a very few of her oldest citizens. The writer of this can go back down the dim aisles of memory only to about the year 1856, and limited in scope as is the retrospective glance, figures and incidents dimmed and softened by the mellowing haze of years, crowd upon his mental vision, emphasizing most strikingly the contrast between the Pensacola of those Arcadian days and the hustling, ambitious little city of the present.
>
> When the writer first knew Pensacola, its population probably did not exceed three thousand souls. Years before, it had been stirred to its depths by the almost assured promise of a railroad running north, and what was locally known as the "New Town" was laid out on paper and speculation in city lots assumed the proportions of a lucrative and permanent vocation.
>
> But the hard times of the thirties nipped that enterprise when it had almost reached the point of fruition, and the "New Town" continued to retain unchanged its characteristic resemblance to a blackjack waste, its primeval aspect modified only by the broken outline of a

Pensacola gained some unwanted national notoriety through the activities of the ardent abolitionist, Jonathan Walker. Walker, a native of Massachusetts, moved his family to Pensacola in 1837 where he treated blacks as equals . . . a practice which offended his slave-holding neighbors. The family returned to Massachusetts in 1843, but Walker came back to Pensacola the following year. On June 22, 1844 he sailed a small boat out of the harbor bound for the British Bahamas. Seven black slaves were aboard the vessel. Walker suffered a sunstroke during the voyage and the boat drifted aimlessly until it was washed up in the Florida Keys. Walker was apprehended and returned to Pensacola where he was charged with stealing slaves. He was once saved from lynching when the sheriff and a deputy, with drawn guns, held off an angry mob. Following a trial, the U. S. District Court judge sentenced him to an hour in the pillory, an additional jail sentence, and to be branded SS for Slave Stealer on the hand. The poet, John Greenleaf Whittier, imprinted the branding on many minds through his poem "The Branded Hand." Photo from Jonathan Walker, *The Trial and Imprisonment of Jonathan Walker* (Facsimile Reproduction, Gainesville: University of Florida Presses, 1974).

United States Marshal branding the author

railroad cut that stretched at intervals through the woods in the direction of Carpenter's Creek.

Intercourse with the outer world was by occasional sailing vessel or steamer with New Orleans and Mobile or by stage across Baldwin County to Blakely [*sic.*], and thence by steamboat to Mobile. Capt. Philip Caro, the father of the present pilots of that name, ran the good schooner *Powhatan*, of about a hundred tons burden, between Pensacola and New Orleans, and in the latter part of the decade of 1850-1860, the little side wheel steamer *Ewing* made daily trips between Milton, Pensacola and the Navy Yard.

In those days the timber business was scarcely in its incipiency. The Bagdad mills and a few others near Milton were in operation, and their product was shipped by an occasional brig or schooner, which generally took cargo at White Point, but with the exception of the 34 war vessels of the United States, which often visited the port, and a few local small craft and the vessels referred to, there was but little in the way of shipping to punctuate the unbroken expanse of the bay. Palafox street wharf, then only a few hundred feet in length, was the only practicable landing place for vessels of any size, and on moonlight evenings it was much in vogue as a promenade for the young gentlemen and ladies of the place. Spanish was spoken almost as universally as English, and the French language was also familiar to most of the people.

What is now Gregory street was practically the northern boundary of the town, there being but few habitations north of it, and Palafox street from Garden north was simply a wagon road bounded on each side by dense titi swamps except at Chase street. The water supply was furnished by three public springs, one in what is now the convent yard, one in the western part of the town and the third about the middle of the square between Garden and Romana and Alcaniz and Tarragona streets. These families that lived any distance from these springs got their daily supply of water in barrels which furnished occupation to one servant for the greater part of the day.

The streets were unlighted at night, and sidewalks were, as a rule, dispensed with except in the heart of the town.

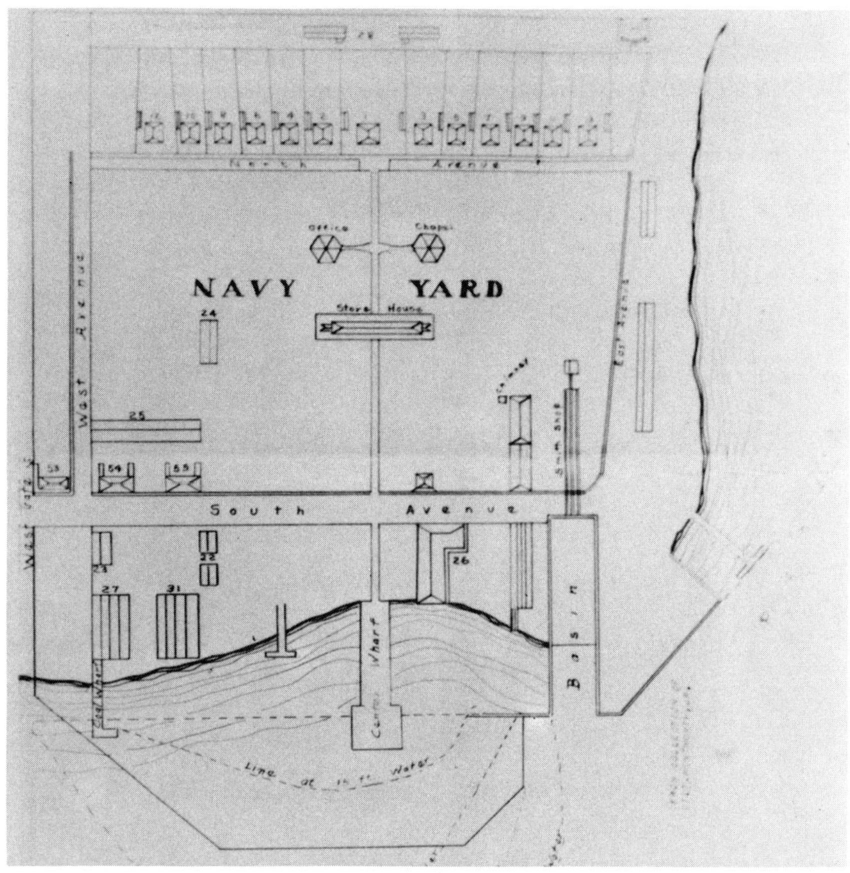

Lieutenant F. B. Renshaw, United States Navy, drew this sketch of the Navy Yard in 1860. The numbers refer to the following buildings: (1) Commodore's Quarters; (2) Commandant's Quarters; (3) Renshaw's Quarters; (4) Quarters of the Second Lieutenant; (5) Surgeon's Quarters; (6) Purser's Quarters; (7) Master's Quarters; (8) Chaplain's Quarters; (9) Assistant Surgeon's Quarters; (10) Constructor; (11) Storekeeper; (12) Commodore's Secretary; (13) Engineer; (17) South Gate; (23) Lime House; (24) Provision House; (25) Warehouse; (26) Store House; (27) Tinder Shed; (28) Stables; (31) Tinder Shed; (53) Marine Quarters; (54) Houses for Boatswain, Gunner; (55) Carpenter and Sail Maker. Photo courtesy of T. T. Wentworth Collection.

Quiet and uneventful as must have been the life of a small community shut off from the busy world as Pensacola then was, it nevertheless was in no sense narrow or mentally contracted. Among the leading citizens were many men and women of culture and refinement; it sustained two newspapers, maintained at least two excellent schools and its members of the bar and other professional men ranked easily on an equality at least, with those of any town in the state.

At long intervals, a minor circus would venture to come here at the risk of pecuniary loss, but as a rule such experiments were few and far between and Pensacolians were content to rely upon Mardi Gras, padgo [*sic.*] shoots, Judas burnings and other home-made entertainments for their diversion.[9]

The Bank of Pensacola began issuing its own currency in 1831. These notes, issued in one, two, three, five, fifty and one hundred dollar denominations, were legal tender in Pensacola. Pensacola Historical Society photo.

12   To Exile And Back

Pensacola was thrust into national prominence as the country prepared for civil war. Both the seceding Southern states and the Union were determined to control Forts Pickens, McRee and Barrancas and the Pensacola Navy Yard. The forts protected the harbor and the navy yard from a sea attack. Control of the harbor either by the state of Florida or by the Confederate States of America would mean that the South would have an open port for the importation of much needed goods. The United States government was determined to see that it retained control of the harbor.

Pensacolians prepared for war. According to Lieutenant Henry Erben, an officer aboard the *USS Supply*, ". . . the people of Pensacola [were] in a state of great excitement . . . the most violent speeches were made to fire the southern heart; men, women, and children seemed to have gone mad."[1] Florida state troops began to converge on Pensacola. Lieutenant Adam Slemmer, the acting commanding officer of Fort Barrancas, posted guards to protect ammunition stores. Shortly before midnight on January 8, 1861, the guards fired warning shots at some shadowy figures near Fort Barrancas. Slemmer claimed that twenty men were seen, but R. L. Sweetman wrote to Slemmer in 1870, stating that there were only two men. Sweetman and another man had been standing on the Fort Barrancas drawbridge. The shots might well have been the first shots of the Civil War fired in defense of the Union.[2]

Florida seceded from the Union on January 10, 1861. Even before the formal organization of the Confederate States of America in Montgomery in February 1861, Florida's Governor Madison Starke Perry ordered the seizure of the forts and the yard. He appointed Colonel William H. Chase, the builder of the forts and now retired from the U. S. Army, to command the Florida State troops. Chase was authorized to seize the forts if he felt certain of success.[3]

Lieutenant Slemmer commanded a small garrison at Fort Barrancas. Fort Pickens had not been garrisoned since 1850 and only a sergeant and his wife served as caretakers for Fort McRee. Slemmer immediately realized his position at Fort Barrancas was indefensible. Indeed, he believed that his meager forces could hold only one fort "and that

Stephen Russell Mallory, born in Trinidad in 1812, grew up in Key West. He received his formal education, which ended when he was seventeen, at a school in Mobile and at an academy in Pennsylvania. He became Inspector of Customs at Key West and read law with Judge William Marvin.

In 1830, Mallory met young Pensacolian, Angela Moreno, eldest daughter of Don Francisco Moreno. After an eight year courtship, he married Angela and settle in Key West where Mallory became active in Democratic politics. In 1850 he was chosen U. S. Senator from Florida and was named to the Senate Naval Affairs Group. He almost singlehandedly began a shipbuilding program which strengthened the Federal Navy for action in the Civil War.

Mallory left the Senate with other Southerners when war began. Because of his naval experience, Confederate President Jefferson Davis appointed him Secretary of the Navy. With limited funds Mallory built a small Confederate Navy which included innovative ironclads.

After the war ended, Mallory practiced law in Pensacola until his death in 1873. Pensacola Historical Society photo.

should be Fort Pickens as it commanded completely the harbor and the forts and also the navy yard."[4]

Slemmer and his forces retreated to Fort Pickens after destroying over 20,000 pounds of powder at Fort McRee and spiking the guns at Fort Barrancas. Seven companies of Alabama and Florida troops occupied the navy yard and Fort Barrancas on January 12, 1861. Colonel Chase immediately demanded the surrender of Fort Pickens. Slemmer refused. Since he had been the builder of Fort Pickens, Chase knew that a land assault on the fort would be costly and would have limited chance of success. Thus, he continued to demand the surrender of the fort without an actual assault and Slemmer continued to refuse.

The Union forces soon had reinforcements available. The sloop *Brooklyn*, with an artillery company commanded by Captain Israel Vogdes embarked, arrived off Fort Pickens. The troops were not landed, however, because a gentlemen's agreement known as the Mallory-Buchanan truce was in effect. This truce, negotiated between Florida's Senator Stephen R. Mallory and President James Buchanan, stated that as long as Fort Pickens was not reinforced, southern troops would not attack it.[5] During the truce Slemmer was allowed to purchase food and to receive mail on the mainland.

The stand-off was still in effect when General Braxton Bragg arrived in Pensacola to take command of the newly organized Confederate troops on March 11, 1861. The situation changed radically in mid-April. Navy Lieutenant John Worden arrived by rail in Pensacola with orders to proceed to Fort Pickens. He assured General Bragg that he had dispatches of a "pacific [*sic.*] nature" for the forces at Fort Pickens. Actually, he carried orders from Secretary of the Navy Gideon Welles which directed the landing of the troops from the *Brooklyn*. These troops were landed on April 12, the same day as the Confederate bombardment of Fort Sumter. The Civil War had begun.[6]

For the next several months Pensacola was tranquil. President Abraham Lincoln ordered all southern ports blockaded on April 19; General Bragg declared martial law in Pensacola on the same day. The two sides endured the monotony of garrison life, the heat of the summer, and mosquitos, fleas and flies. Their boredom was briefly relieved in May when the Confederates tried to move a large floating dry-dock from the navy yard to Pensacola. The tow line broke and, as the dock drifted close to Fort Pickens, Federal forces readied their cannon to fire upon the floating target. They were thwarted when the Confederates scuttled the dry-dock.[7]

Company B of the 9th Mississippi encamped near Fort Barrancas cook over an open fire. Uniform regulations appear to be lax. Library of Congress photo.

The fall brought more action. In September the Confederates began outfitting the privateer *Judah*. When the Federals discovered this activity they planned to destroy the vessel before she could put to sea. On the night of September 14 a small force of sailors and marines boarded the *Judah* and set her afire. They also spiked the guns of the battery which was protecting the vessel.[8]

General Bragg immediately decided upon a retaliatory measure: Confederate forces would take Fort Pickens. During the night of October 9, Confederate troops under General Richard Anderson crossed the bay to Santa Rosa Island and landed about four miles east of the fort. They trudged through the soft sand for about three miles before being spotted by a picket of the 6th New York Regiment. After a brief skirmish the 6th New York retreated to Fort Pickens and alerted the troops there of the attack. Since dawn was nearing and the Federals were massing to attack his troops, General Anderson ordered a general retreat. The Battle of Santa Rosa Island ended when the Confederate forces reboarded their steamers and sailed back to Pensacola.[9]

The monotony of garrison life resumed, punctuated by artillery duels between Fort Pickens and Fort Barrancas. In November of 1861 the thundering guns shook the houses of Pensacola and inflicted minor damage to both forts. The second major artillery battle, on January 1 and 2, 1862, caused extensive damage to the navy yard and blew up the powder magazine at Fort McRee.[10] Ironically, the only time the cannon of the forts were fired in anger was not to defend the entrance to the harbor, but rather at each other. When the guns finally fell silent both garrisons once again settled into the dull routine of camp life.

As Pensacola's role in the Civil War declined, events farther north had a profound effect upon the city. In February 1862 General Bragg was ordered to take four regiments to join the Army of Tennessee. The evacuation proceeded slowly as Bragg's men set about destroying everything they could not take with them. The navy yard was stripped of valuable machinery and the Confederate's last act was to set fires at Fort Barrancas, Fort McRee and the marine hospital. The final withdrawal began on May 7 and took two days. A token garrison under the command of Confederate Colonel Thomas M. Jones remained in the city. Acting Mayor Dr. John Brosnaham finally surrendered Pensacola to Lieutenant Richard Jackson of the U. S. Army on May 10, 1862.[11]

During and after the Confederate evacuation Pensacolians fled the city in droves, leaving less than one hundred people behind. Union troops occupied Seville Square and used Old Christ Church as a stable. In the early morning hours the troops marched up and down the square singing patriotic songs. Their activity was observed by one of the few remaining Pensacola families: that of Spanish Consul Don Francisco Moreno. During the marching activity one of Moreno's daughters loudly sang southern songs in the parlor. The Moreno parrot added to the concert by singing "The Bonnie Blue Flag." When Union officers called on Moreno to protest this activity the Spanish consul professed embarrassment; but he later rewarded the parrot with a biscuit.[12]

Most of the people who fled the city evacuated to either Montgomery or Greenville, Alabama. In a unique legislative act the Florida Legislature authorized Pensacola's Board of Aldermen to transact business outside the corporate limits. All records were removed—first to Bluff Springs and then to Greenville, Alabama where Pensacola city business was transacted between the middle of 1862 and 1865. Exiled Pensacolians even bought and sold Pensacola property through the

*The attack on Wilson's camp began the Battle of   photo from an engraving in Harper's Weekly, 7
Santa Rosa Island. Pensacola Historical Society   December 1861.*

government at Greenville.[13]

Pensacola was now an occupied city. Some troops were quartered in the Seville Square area and a force varying from 1,800 to 3,000 men garrisoned Fort Barrancas. Union forces also occupied the navy yard. Although no major action took place during these years of occupation, troops from Barrancas engaged in several skirmishes with roving Confederate bands in and around Escambia County. Union soldiers raided surrounding farms, frequently hauling away the family piano, thus giving the name "Piano Raids" to their activities.[14]

The raids and skirmishes created a refugee problem as people fled to the protection of Fort Barrancas. Eventually more than 2,000 soldiers and civilians camped in a small area near the fort creating a "Shack Town." The civilians, labeled "destitute and homeless," received food and building supplies from the garrison. When the war ended some of them moved into the city of Pensacola, joining the exiled Pensacolians who began to return to their city.[15]

Immediately after the war times were hard and money was scarce. Only four families could claim furniture valued at more than $600.[16] Pensacolians resented the military occupation by Union troops and the hardships imposed by the Reconstruction Acts.

The formal period of Reconstruction was relatively short-lived in Pensacola as compared to other areas of the defeated South. When Congress began enacting the Reconstruction Laws Florida became part of the Third Military District, commanded by General George Meade. The Pensacola District was commanded by Major General Truman Seymour, "a man of strong prejudices, with a tendency to impulsive action."[17]

Pensacola was under military rule until 1868 when Florida adopted a new constitution acceptable to the U. S. Congress. During and after the period of military rule many newly freed Negroes came to Pensacola, seeking help from the Freedman's Bureau. When General Meade proclaimed the Constitution of 1868 to be "the supreme law of Florida" he suspended military rule.[18] The army continued, however, to control some activities. Seymour's successor, Colonel Henry S. Gansevoort wrote to his father in August 1868, describing his duties:

> I have charge of quarantine and of the army reserve extending for several miles, am in command of five counties, Walton, Holmes, Escambia, Santa Rosa and Washington. In these counties, I am errecting [*sic.*], or at least in three of

them, schoolhouses, with slight appropriation of materials and the voluntary labor of the people. I therefore have to contract for materials and be responsible for considerable funds.

Then I have to dispense rations, or rather sign ration returns, for each destitute in these five counties as appear to be most deserving. These receive on such returns from the commissary or subsistence certain amounts of subsistence stores. In this way many poor persons, both white and black, are supported.[19]

Pensacola began to rebuild. By the end of the terrible decade of the 1860s Pensacola was on the verge of an economic boom.

"Gen. [Neal] Dow, while in command at Pensacola had discovered a great fondness for pianos and miscellaneous articles of furniture, of which he had a large and interesting collection at his quarters. Numerous predatory raids had been made into the adjoining towns; and when we reached Pensacola it was said that the looting had been so effective that but little if any valuable furniture was left in all Western Florida. Subsequently, near Port Hudson, this pseudo General was taken prisoner. It was reported that the rebels offered to exchange him for six pianos, but the proposition seems not to have been accepted, and he was, I believe, afterwards exchanged in the regular way." Wm. C. Holbrook, *A Narrative of the Services of the Officers and Enlisted Men of the 7th Regiment of Vermont Volunteers From 1862 to 1865* (New York: American Bank Note Co., 1882), 11. Pensacola Historical Society photo.

13   Boom Town

As the decade of the 1870s opened Pensacola began to change from the sleepy, backwoods town which it had been almost from its founding. Three economic elements came together at a propitious time to make Pensacola a boom town.

First, the all-important rail connection to Montgomery was completed in the winter of 1870. The Pensacola and Louisville Railroad Company connected with the Mobile and Montgomery Railroad at Pensacola Junction (Flomaton). This link provided connections to the burgeoning railroad system of the South. It eventually became part of the vast Louisville and Nashville Railroad system and gave Pensacola land access to markets in the North.[1]

Building an east-west railroad presented difficult problems. Vast areas of pineland, cut by rivers and streams, had to be traversed if Pensacola were to have railroad connections to other parts of Florida. The Pensacola and Atlantic Railroad began construction of a line between Pensacola and Jacksonville in June 1881. Working during the heat of summer and through the frosts of winter, track layers and bridge builders finally completed the line in the spring of 1883. On April 11, 1883, P & A President Fred DeFuniak announced, "today we witness the entire line completed in a thoroughly first-class manner. . . . The heavy grades near the different streams, the long and costly structures which cross them, the high price of labor and material when the work was let, and the rapidity with which the work was accomplished, all combine to furnish grounds for congratulations upon the cost and manner in which the work has been completed."[2]

The new railroads and the old port of Pensacola became inextricably joined when the former built wharves along the waterfront. The Pensacola and Louisville first constructed a 2,000 foot wharf along the bay.[3] In the ensuing years, the Louisville and Nashville owned three wharves: Commendencia Street, Tarragona Street and Muscogee. Other wharves were privately owned and included Herron's, Palafox, Central and Sullivan's.[4]

Why so many wharves in what had been essentially a military town? The answer was *Lumber.* As the country expanded, the demand for

The harvesting of pitch and tar came as a by-product of the lumber boom. Collectively known as naval stores, these products from pine trees were used aboard sailing ships. Soon turpentine and resin were added to products known as naval stores. Resin, the residue of gum turpentine distillation, was extracted by a "streak" tapped or chipped on the face of the tree. An "apron" or "gutter" of galvanized iron in a V shape was nailed to the tree to guide the gum into the "cup." "Dipping" crews collected the gum for processing by the distillery or "still." Distillation of turpentine, although not new to the area, developed as an industry after the Civil War and turpentine camps were situated throughout West Florida. In 1895, A. M. Moses and Company opened resin and turpentine yards in the Pensacola area. In 1902 when pine became scarce due to the lumber boom, crews extracted resin from stumps of cut-down trees. The industry received a major boost in 1916 when Newport Industries located a plant in Pensacola for the production of naval stores. Pensacola Historical Society photo.

Bay front crews loaded lumber aboard ships through holes cut near the waterline. As the weighted vessel sank lower in the water, old holes were patched and new ones cut for additional loading. T. T. Wentworth Collection photo.

timber grew, bringing to national attention the great stretches of longleaf pine forests in Northwest Florida and Southern Alabama. Longleaf pine, the most valuable of the southern pines, grew tall with scant foliage except at the crown. The trees were almost solid hardwood with very little waste in excess branches and, thus, were the preferred wood for construction.[5]

By 1880 logging operations in northwest Florida were in full swing. The sound of crosscut saws was heard throughout the area. Once the tree was felled, it was cut into logs which were sometimes hand-hewn. The logs were hauled by oxen to streams or to the railroad for the long trip to one of the many mills which dotted the area. Once at the mill, the logs were fashioned into boards and readied for shipment either by rail or by ship.[6]

Ships from all over the world came into Pensacola harbor to load lumber. A visitor described the harbor in 1884: "There were schooners, brigs, barks, and ships from Russia, Denmark, Germany, England, France, Spain, Norway, Italy and Australia. The principal business of these vessels is carrying lumber."[7] In 1887 alone, 518 vessels entered the bay, 361 of these were from foreign ports. Their principal cargo was lumber, but cotton and pig iron were also loaded aboard the ships.[8]

Most of the ships entered the harbor in ballast; their holds were filled with rocks, tile, sand and gravel from all over the world.[9] Since an empty ship tends to capsize, the ballast was used to stabilize the sailing vessels during the long voyage across the Atlantic. When the ship entered port the ballast was dumped to make room for the cargo.

During the summer months when epidemics seemed to occur, the ballast was off-loaded at the Quarantine Station at Deer Point. The Quarantine Station had been established to control the spread of yellow fever and other diseases associated with the arrival of ships from foreign ports. Although the true cause of yellow fever was not known at that time, physicians suspected that it could be spread by an infected person. Ships were fumigated at the Quarantine Station and the crew examined for signs of the disease.[10]

The ballast from the ships was dumped into specially constructed cribs. The first crib at the Quarantine Station cost $4,500 and was 200 feet by 150 feet. It was expanded in size between 1884 and 1886 as more ballast was dumped into it.[11] Similar cribs were built around the shoreline of the bay at Pensacola. The cribs were made of heavy timber bolted together with one inch bolts and divided into "apartments" each about 12 by 15 feet and reaching from the bottom to about four or five feet above the water. Sometimes the ships were moored to the cribs but this was not always a safe procedure, particularly during storms.[12]

E. E. Saunders obtained a lucrative contract to off-load the ballast from ships tied up to the piers. He would then sell the ballast to road builders. Since each vessel's owner had to pay for off-loading ballast, there was frequent illegal dumping along the shoreline. Almost sixty acres of high, dry land was created by five million tons of ballast dumped along the shore by ships from all over the world.[13]

Not only did Pensacola grow in geographic size during this period, it also grew in population as people from many parts of Europe came to the port city. Ethnic communities sprouted up all over the city. "Little

Apache Chief Geronimo came involuntarily to Pensacola in 1886. He had surrendered to General Nelson A. Miles in Arizona and was a prisoner of war. Pensacolians Sewell C. Cobb and William and Louis Knowles wanted Geronimo and his band imprisoned at Fort Pickens where they would be a tourist attraction. They petitioned President Grover Cleveland to send the Apaches to Pensacola. Although ridiculed by some, the request solved the problem of Geronimo's imprisonment for President Cleveland. Pensacola headlines blared: "Geronimo Coming."

When the band arrived at the depot a large crowd greeted the Indians who were taken to the fort by steamer and housed in the casemates. During the next two years, thousands of visitors went by boat to Fort Pickens to view the Apaches. Many young Pensacola women wanted to bestow gifts upon Geronimo and his followers. Soldiers guarding the band discouraged gifts; one said, "the best thing you could give him would be an ounce of lead between the eyes."

Pensacola's chapter in the Geronimo story ended in May 1888 when the Apaches were taken to Mount Vernon. Woodward B. Skinner, *Geronimo at Fort Pickens* (Pensacola: Frank Parkhurst and Son, 1981). Pensacola Historical Society photo.

In 1869 Sewell Cobb shipped a cargo of red snapper north and a new industry was born in Pensacola. Ice was the key to its success. With the development of refrigerated railroad cars, fish could be shipped long distances. In 1885 more than three million tons of fish were shipped from Pensacola. Saunders Company and Warren Fish Company, two of the largest shippers of fish, owned fleets of boats and hired fishing crews. Often, these men found themselves "volunteered" to fish after a night in town bars. Beer and whiskey were loaded aboard the ships and given to the crew to prevent what was called "the horrors." Captain Max Alford of the John Francis Turner *explained: "The crew have all been drinking for a week. Some of them longer . . . If they're cut off too suddenly some of them are apt to go into the horrors and we'd have to chain them from jumping overboard or hurting themselves." Wyatt Blassingame, "They Sail From Hangover Harbor,"* True: Fishing Year-book *(1958), 52-53, 88-90.*

Fishing boats first had open wells filled with sea water to keep fresh caught-seafood from spoiling. The smacking sound of the water in the wells gave the boats the name, "fishing smacks." When the industry began, the best most fertile waters were within fifteen miles of Pensacola Bay. As these grounds were over-fished, the smacks ventured farther into the Gulf for red snapper. Men lined the sides of the boats using large fishing poles to haul in the catch. When the ship returned to the harbor, the fish were loaded either aboard larger vessels or railroad cars for shipment. Soon, Pensacola became known as the "Red Snapper Capital of the World." Pensacola Historical Society photo.

Italy" grew up between Barcelona and Coyle streets from Garden to Main. "Little Norway" extended from A to G streets south of Main Street. The Scandinavian Missionary Society of Norway sponsored a church near the waterfront as early as 1870. Services were conducted by a Scandinavian minister and a reading room was stocked with Scandinavian books and newspapers.[14]

Greeks came to Pensacola from the island of Skopelos and remained to form a large Greek community. Many were bachelors hoping to earn money for a sister's dowry. These men married Greek women from Skopelos. Some of the Greeks became fishermen working on the snapper smacks, others operated small grocery stores. Their traditions and culture were preserved through the Greek Orthodox Church which opened in 1910.[15]

Retail businesses were operated by German Jews. Although the Jews participated in business and community activities, they kept to themselves after working hours and centered their lives around the Temple and a social organization called the Progress Club. In 1900 Temple Beth-El was located on Chase street where many Jewish people also lived.[16]

Only one ethnic group had to cope with an identity crisis. Pensacola's Creoles were people whose ancestry was a blend of Spanish, French, Canary Islanders, former slaves and others. They lived near their church, St. Joseph's Catholic Church, and kept themselves aloof from the black population. In 1900 this group was secure in professional, artisan and service positions. Many were barbers. The City Directory classified them as "white" or "Creole." In 1910 the term "Creole" disappeared from the City Directory and the Creoles were forced to choose between calling themselves white or black. Creoles, however, still tended to stay together and to regard themselves as a distinct cultural entity.[17]

The black population of Pensacola was economically divided into a thriving middle class and laborers. Successful black men included John Sunday, who served in the Florida Legislature in 1874 and as a city alderman from 1878 to 1881; D. J. Cunningham, who operated the Excelsior Grocery in 1895; and Thomas DeSalle Tucker, an attorney. Alexander Plummer, a black entrepreneur, invested in black-owned businesses. Black residential neighborhoods sprang up along the railroad tracks near the main business district and southwest of North Hill.[18]

"Jim Crow" came late to the city compared to the rest of the south.

During the lumber boom Sarah Bernhardt, George M. Cohan, Helena Modjeska, Billie Burke and Maude Adams and hundreds of lesser luminaries appeared at the Pensacola Opera House. The ornate Victorian building on the southeast corner of Jefferson and Government Streets opened January 4, 1883. Despite its name, few if any Grand Operas were heard at the Opera House. Popular attractions included Shakespearean plays and dramatic works. Turn-of-the-century Pensacolians of all social classes made the Opera House popular during the height of the lumber boom. Opera House popularity declined as movie houses began to draw audiences to the new entertainment medium. The great building was destroyed by a storm on September 28, 1917 and was never restored. Pensacola Historical Society photo.

During the 1870s and 1880s William Dudley Chipley became the biggest promoter for Pensacola. In 1877 Chipley printed a pamphlet, Pensacola: The Naples of America *touting the city for tourists, industries and anyone else who wished to come to the city. Though he wrote the tract as part of a promotional campaign for the railroad interests, he firmly believed that Pensacola was the finest little city in the south.*

Chipley, born in Columbus, Georgia, grew up in Lexington, Kentucky where his father was a Baptist minister. He fought for the South during the Civil War. Returning to Columbus after the war, he worked for the Georgia Railroad and was active in Democratic politics. He moved to Pensacola to become general manager of the Pensacola and Louisville Railroad which eventually became part of the Louisville and Nashville Railroad. Chipley was instrumental in obtaining railroad connections to the north and the east. He worked to have the channel deepened for steamers and to have the Navy Yard reopened after the Civil War. Chipley's leadership contributed to the growth of the city during the late nineteenth century. A monument to this "Father of Modern Pensacola" stands in Plaza Ferdinand. Pensacola Historical Society photo.

The eight-story Hotel San Carlos opened on February 1, 1910, billed as one of the most modern hotels in the south. Located at Palafox and Garden Streets across from the Blount Building, the Spanish-style edifice enhanced the city's major downtown intersection. Tourists, travelling businessmen and Pensacolians enjoyed the comforts of the dining room and ballroom. The hotel remained a focal point for Pensacola society until the 1970s. The hotel was closed in 1981. In the 1980s it was a focus for downtown restoration.

The impressive structure on the southwest corner of Palafox and Garden Streets has been known as both the Blount and the Brent Building. W. A. Blount and his son, architect F. M. Blount, began construction in 1906. Meanwhile, F. C. Brent was erecting a building just south of the Blount Building. The three-story, fire-proof Brent Building was completed in 1907. In 1908 Blount sold his seven-story structure to the Brent interests and the two buildings began to be collectively known as the Brent Building. Later, the name reverted to the Blount Building. By whatever name it is called, the building remains a major landmark at Palafox and Garden. Pensacola Historical Society photo.

The lack of certain discriminations was probably due to the prosperous lumber boom. Jobs were readily available and blacks and whites did not have to compete against each other for them. As the lumber industry declined, this situation changed. Jim Crow laws were enacted and blacks suffered the same discriminatory practices used elsewhere in the South.[19]

School segregation had been a fact of life for Pensacola's black children. Prior to the Constitution of 1868 there were no provisions for any black schools. Schools for whites had been under the supervision of the Registrar of Land Affairs. The 1868 Constitution provided, for the first time, for a State Superintendent of Education. Local public schools were established and grew in number from old Public School No. 1 to eight white and eight black schools in 1905.[20] A strong private school system also existed in both the black and white communities. The teachers usually taught in their homes or in church buildings. The Pensacola Classical School attracted students from the more prosperous white families. As the city grew in area more public schools were opened in outlying areas.[21]

In the early years of the twentieth century Pensacola experienced a building boom. In 1905 the entire business section on Palafox Street, from Garden to Romana, was destroyed by fire. Re-building began immediately. Within a month after the fire F. C. Brent negotiated a contract for a three-story fireproof building at Garden and Palafox streets. W. A. Blount erected a seven story fireproof building and, in 1906, the First National Bank completed a building which resembled a Greek Temple. A new City Hall was constructed on Jefferson Street in 1908. And, in 1910, the magnificent Hotel San Carlos opened for business. Between 1906 and 1909 nearly $3,000,000 dollars were spent on building construction in downtown Pensacola.[22]

As the downtown grew, so did the residential areas. Wealthy Pensacolians lived in the elegant North Hill area. East Hill became the home of a prosperous middle class. With the coming of the "street railway system" in 1902 people began to live farther from their work. New residential areas opened in East Pensacola Heights, the Lakeview subdivision and Brownsville.[23] A "Dummy Line" (the cars were pulled by a "dummy motor," a steam engine disguised as a streetcar) took people from Pensacola to the navy yard via the Bayshore.[24]

The twentieth century also brought a decline in the great lumber boom. The vast forests of Escambia and Santa Rosa Counties were almost clear-cut. One old timer described how the devastated land

Modeste Hargis, daughter of Dr. Robert Bell Smith Hargis, was Florida's first woman pharmacist. In 1912 the Hargis Pharmacy, known as "The Little Drug Store Around the Corner," was located in the American National Bank Building on the northwest corner of Palafox and Government Streets. Interview with Elizabeth Vickers, 1985. Pensacola Historical Society photo.

looked: ". . . It was like some huge scar that wouldn't heal. There wasn't any wildlife to speak of . . . just that gullied brown ground, and a sick feeling the whole thing needn't have happened."[25] As the distances between the pine forests and the port lengthened, lumbering became more and more unprofitable. There were no plans for reforestation and the great stands of longleaf pines disappeared. By 1910 Pensacola's great lumber boom was over.

14 THE MOTHER-IN-LAW OF THE NAVY

For almost fifty years following the Civil War the military presence in Pensacola was eclipsed by the great lumber boom. The army reservation, colloquially known as "Barrancas," comprised nearly 1,700 acres west of the Pensacola Navy Yard. The area contained Fort Barrancas, the Advanced Redoubt and the Post of Fort Barrancas. Six officers and one hundred twenty five enlisted men garrisoned the post. The men lived in the largest building on the post: Barrancas Barracks. Officers were quartered in houses which surrounded the parade field. Four of these homes had been built before the Civil War and six others had been constructed by 1875. All but the old commandant's house, which burned in the 1960s, still remain inhabited today.[1]

The old navy yard never fully recovered from the devastations of the Civil War. Although it was designed to repair and outfit ships of the Gulf Squadron, little work of this sort was done at the yard. The commandant's quarters, which was completed in 1874, was situated on a tree-lined street within the brick wall that surrounded the yard.[2] This house and street symbolized the relaxed lifestyle of the naval officers during the 1870s and 1880s. Naval authorities considered closing the yard as early as the 1880s. Efforts to save it were successful but there was still very little naval activity in Pensacola.

When the Spanish-American War broke out in 1898 patriotic Pensacolians believed that "Pensacola was the natural site for troop embarkation and a base of supplies for the forces operating against Cuba (and would thereby also reap economic gains from the war)."[3] When Tampa was chosen as the embarkation port Pensacolians were naturally disappointed. The disappointment did not prevent them for volunteering for military service. Men of the First Battalion of Florida's naval militia drilled at the navy yard. Even though the Pensacola Navy Yard did not play a significant role in the war, some long overdue repairs were made at the yard because of the war and the navy acquired a small wooden dry dock.[4]

Pensacola's army facilities also benefited from the war. The Post of Fort Barrancas was the headquarters for the Coast Artillery Corps which defended the harbor. Construction of reinforced concrete plat-

This aerial view of the Naval Air Station taken in 1922 depicts Chevalier Field (center) located on the site of the village of Woolsey. Old Warrington forms the background to the west of the station. The Air Station had already outgrown the original northern boundaries of the Navy Yard; growth to the west was inevitable. Pensacola Historical Society photo.

forms for Battery Pensacola, located in the center of the Fort Pickens, cas, began in 1898. The battery was armed with two 12-inch seacoast cannon mounted on disappearing carriages. On June 20, 1899, eight thousand pounds of powder blew up as fire swept over the northwest bastion of the fort. The explosion ripped a hole in the northwest bastion which was never repaired. A concrete road was laid through the hole which made it easier to get to Battery Pensacola.[5]

After the war Pensacola's military facilities again lapsed into obscurity. The Coast Artillery continued to garrison the Post of Fort Barrancas. But fears that the Pensacola Navy Yard would close persisted. A floating wooden drydock, purchased from Spain in 1902, was towed to Pensacola and people hoped that new shipbuilding and repair work would rejuvenate the old yard. Unfortunately, the drydock was destroyed by the 1906 hurricane.

The yard was finally closed on 20 October 1911. Fort Barrancas was sparsely garrisoned and it looked as though, for the first time in its history, Pensacola would have no established military community.[6]

This unwelcome development came just as the lumber industry was declining and Pensacola was in the throes of a recession. The Pensacola State Bank closed in December 1913 and in January 1914, the First National Bank closed. City leaders thought that modernization of the naval establishment would be a partial solution to the economic crisis. The infant Navy Air Arm was looking for a permanent base to use for training pilots. Mayor Adolph Greenhut and members of the City Council actively encouraged the Navy to locate its training at the old navy yard. Greenhut said that the Navy would add thousands of dollars to local businesses.[7]

Fortunately the board of naval officers appointed to "draw up" a comprehensive plan for the organization of a "Naval Aeronautic Service" also thought Pensacola would be the best place to establish the Naval Air Training Station.[8] On January 20, 1914, nine officers and twenty-three enlisted men arrived in Pensacola to establish a flying school. They brought with them seven aircraft and some portable hangars. Construction activity at the old navy yard created jobs for Pensacolians and as more instructors and flight students arrived, Pensacola's economy had a new influx of money.

The naval aviators stationed at Pensacola entered into the social life of the city. The 1915 Mardi Gras celebration featured the arrival of King Priscus XVI in a plane piloted by Lieutenant W. McIlvain, United States Marine Corps. The young ladies of Pensacola found the naval aviators socially attractive. At this time, Pensacola began to earn the sobriquet "Mother-in-law of the Navy." Only one class of fliers who graduated between 1914 and 1923 left Pensacola without a Pensacola bride. By 1931 more than one hundred Pensacola women had married naval or marine officers.[9]

The number of student pilots increased dramatically when the United States entered World War I. Almost 1,000 aviators completed flight training betwen April 1917 and November 1918. Construction of new facilities for men and equipment enlarged the station beyond the original wall of the old navy yard. Local contractors and local firms provided new jobs and salaries for civilians soared. In 1917 the Navy

Ned Wyer's Silver Cornet Band provided entertainment for many Pensacola events in the early part of the twentieth century. Pensacola Historical Society photo.

The Pensacola Shipbuilding Company was active in ship construction during and immediately after World War I. Pensacola Historical Society photo.

spent as much as $400,000 a month on construction at the station.

A housing shortage developed as the result of an influx of workers and military personnel. The *Pensacola Journal* on January 3, 1918 declared that "the city is a barracks for servicemen." Pensacolians rented rooms to some of these people and, in later years, servicemen recalled the generosity of the city.[10]

World War I also brought another industry to Pensacola. The Pensacola Shipbuilding Company began building ships at its site on Bayou Chico. The fifteen hundred workers at the shipyard needed housing and better transportation. In 1918 the federal government spent three quarters of a million dollars for housing units between "H" and "O"

The Newport Company on O Street (now Pace Boulevard) is now part of the Reichold Chemical Company. Pensacola Historical Society photo.

streets south of Chase. The Escambia County Commission authorized installation of a lift bridge over Bayou Chico. Together, the Pensacola Naval Air Station and the Pensacola Shipbuilding Company added ten thousand people to the city's population in two years.[11]

Only one other industry fueled Pensacola's economy at this time and it probably sneaked into the city on a ruse. Old timers say that in 1916 the Newport Company, a manufacturer of naval stores, bought land west of the city ostensibly for a chicken farm. Conservative city leaders believed that industry in the city would destroy its charm. But, soon after the land purchase more than 200 workers at the new plant processed over 150 tons of wood per day into turpentine and resins.[12]

By the end of World War I Pensacola's economy was firmly based on the activities of the Pensacola Naval Air Station. Although there were other small industries in and around the city, the United States government was the largest civilian employer in the area. Efforts to make the port competitive with Mobile and New Orleans failed, primarily because of the lack of a major river flowing into the bay.

15 THE ROARING TWENTIES AND DEPRESSING THIRTIES

Even before the end of World War I Pensacola began to experience disasters. The first came in the form of disease . . . not the old, dreaded yellow fever, which had been eradicated, but from influenza. So many died from the disease in the fall of 1918 and funeral processions became so numerous that the survivors often suffered from depression.[1]

Unemployment also came as the Navy cut back activities when the war ended. The Newport Company closed its plant for most of 1921 due to "unstable market conditions."[2] The port was not recovering from its wartime slump.

The "hard times" did not last very long. Pensacola began to recover economically by 1922 partly because of the general Florida land boom. Land sales escalated and developers opened new subdivisions. Road building throughout Escambia County improved the deplorable road situation which had existed in pre-war Pensacola. At last residents could travel over paved highways instead of sandy roads. Ferries went out of business as bridges were built across Escambia Bay, Perdido Bay near Lillian Highway and, finally, Pensacola Bay.[3]

Economic dependence on the Naval Air Station continued. The *Pensacola Journal* on June 28, 1928 called the station, "the city's most important commercial asset." Between 400 and 700 civilians were annually employed by the navy. "At that time the Naval Air Station was probably contributing between one-fourth [and] one-fifth of the total salaries in Pensacola."[4]

The roads, bridges and the continued influx of naval officers from other parts of the country continued to change Pensacola from a sleepy, semi-rural town to a small cosmopolitan city. The foundations for these changes had been laid during the lumber boom when hundreds of immigrants settled in Pensacola. The spirit of the twenties fueled this change.

Automobiles came to Pensacola before World War I, but the impact of this new vehicle altered the town both socially and economically during the 1920s. Dependency upon public transportation waned as more people bought automobiles. New residential areas grew beyond

Opening of the three-mile Pensacola Bay Bridge in 1931 spurred an emerging tourist business. The Bay Bridge and the bridge across Santa Rosa Sound provided road access to Pensacola Beach. On the beach the new Casino gave tourists and Pensacolians a place to change clothes, to eat and even to dance. The two-lane bridge was replaced in the 1960s by a more modern four-lane roadway. The old bridge, minus its center section, is now used as a fishing pier. Pensacola Historical Society photo.

the old city limits. Automobiles had an effect upon women's cloths; long skirts were difficult to manage when driving a car. The changing fashions brought the "new woman" to Pensacola as some of the local belles embraced the flapper image.

Entertainment took on a new form as movies began to be shown in the Saenger, Isis and Bonita theaters. Radio in the form of WCOA officially came to the town in 1926. Dance bands abounded as did bootleggers. Sam Clepper, a noted bootlegger, became a legendary figure. Although he was frequently jailed for his illegal activities, he managed to avoid conviction for years. During his brief incarcerations in the town jail his customers brought him food from their own kitchens. "Jail food was not good for anyone and we wanted to keep Sam healthy."[5]

The great party ended suddenly. No one in Pensacola was prepared for the crash of 1929 and the depression which followed. At first, the city did not feel the disastrous effects of the crash. The Navy had begun a building program in 1929 and 1930 and the civilian payroll actually increased between 1929 and 1931. Pensacolians congratulated themselves on having escaped the worst of the nation-wide depression.

The family car became an institution during the 1920s and 1930s. This vehicle from the 1920s is proudly parked in front of the T. C. Watson residence on Gregory Street. The house is an example of the rococco Victorian style favored by builders and residents of North Hill. Pensacola Historical Society photo.

They soon learned that they had not escaped. In 1931 store owners witnessed a decline in sales. The Naval Air Station had no new construction of any magnitude. A local survey reported that more than 4,000 persons were unemployed in the summer of 1931. An Unemployment Relief Committee was organized and many families were totally dependent on funds provided by this committee. The newspapers featured many more ads under "Situations Wanted" than there were

The Wisteria Cafeteria, 28 N. Palafox Street, was a favorite gathering place for Pensacola High School Students. Pensacola Historical Society photo.

job offers. A hobo city grew up near the L & N tracks at 17th Avenue. By 1933 Pensacola was suffering as much as other areas of the country.

Private citizens and groups tried to help those in need. The Kiwanis Club maintained a medical clinic for poor children; the Elks gave fifty pound Christmas boxes to 500 families in 1931 and 1932; Parent-Teacher Associations contributed food to hungry students. Black residents had their own Community Chest drive in 1931 and a group of more prosperous blacks, known as "The Invincible Twenty," engaged in charitable activities in the black community.

The Roosevelt administration initiated legislation to help the poor and needy. Local relief agencies enrolled applicants for both welfare and work relief under the Federal Emergency Relief Act. Work relief crews, who were paid thirty cents an hour, improved the drainage system on Baylen Street, built the 17th Avenue underpass and widened many streets including Barrancas Avenue from Garden Street to Bayou Chico.[6]

When work relief projects were switched to the Civil Works Administration, almost 3,000 Pensacolians participated in the $50,000 a year payroll. The viaduct on Cervantes Street was built during the six months that the CWA existed. It cost $300,000 and gave work to nearly one hundred men.[7]

The Works Project Administration became the major work-relief organization in the late thirties. WPA employment in Pensacola varied from 600 in 1938 to 1,700 in 1939. Construction projects included Bayou Texar Boulevard, O Street, Lakeview Avenue and the completion of Barrancas Avenue from Bayou Chico to Bayou Grande.

The WPA also engaged in educational activities among the poor and illiterate. The Chairman of the Escambia County Board of Commissioners John N. Rauscher stated:

> Hundreds of illiterate adults in Pensacola and Escambia County have been taught to read and write. Aliens have been taught and prepared for citizenship. Child care and child welfare work has been conducted, particularly among mothers. Classes in Health and Sanitation among the underprivileged have been conducted and living conditions in many homes have been improved as a result of the Adult Education Program. Classes in Reading, Writing, Arithmetic, English and other common branches have been conducted among borderline adults with wonderful results . . .[8]

As the depression decade drew to a close, many Pensacolians were still living at the poverty level. According to the 1940 census, only half of Pensacola's 8,376 residential structures had a private bath and a private flush toilet. A little over one third of the homes used electricity for refrigeration and less than three-fourths of the homes had a radio.[9]

Public housing projects opened to residents in 1940. Camelia Court, later called Attucks Court, on West Cervantes was occupied by black tenants and Azalea, later Aragon Court, housed low income white families Another public housing project, Moreno Court, located just east of Corry Field, was the most expensive of these projects, costing over $600,000.[10]

Like the rest of the country, Pensacola was recovering from the

This Greek restaurant on Main Street was a popular place for members of Pensacola's Greek community. Pensacola Historical Society photo.

depression when the war in Europe gave new impetus to the military installations in the area. Both the WPA and PWA programs had been used to construct additional buildings aboard the Naval Air Station. Corry Field had opened in 1927 and by 1938 fifteen auxilliary fields operated in the Pensacola area.[11]

16   War Changes The City

Pensacola was as shocked as the rest of the nation by the Japanese bombing of Pearl Harbor on December 7, 1941. On the following day thirty-five men from Pensacola enlisted in the armed forces of the United States. More men "joined up" during the next few months. Bill Bond, who was a 1940 graduate of Pensacola High School and later a turret gunner on a B-24 bomber, expressed the emotions of his age group:

> We thought Japs lived in paper houses and that a match would burn down Tokyo. We had been taught pride in country, loyalty, and dedication and the superiority of the U. S. Then FDR spoke of that 'dastardly deed' in his inspiring way and we (I, anyway) had goose bumps and thought there is no way those Japs are going to survive. We young men had no hang-ups about serving. We wanted to go and, if anything, were afraid we might be left behind. One boy was late for the bus to carry civilians to army camp and ran up in a panic that he might miss it.[1]

On December 8, 1941 the Pensacola City Council placed the entire city on an emergency basis "for the duration." Emergency measures included air and fire warden service, the augmentation of the police force by American Legion members, guarding the water supply against possible sabotage and experiments with "black-outs."[2]

Within nine days following the declaration of war the flight training schedule at the Naval Air Station jumped from enrolling 800 students a year to an enrollment figure of 2,500 per year. This figure continued to increase and by war's end over 27,000 naval aviators had been trained at Pensacola Naval Air Station.[3]

As the navy's role in Pensacola expanded, the role of the army diminished. The need for coastal harbor defense waned as the war progressed, and, one by one, units of the Thirteenth Coast Artillery, stationed at Fort Barrancas, were ordered overseas. In 1947 the navy acquired the old Post of Fort Barrancas and the Naval Schools of

Sailors guard an airplane engine used to promote one of the many War Bond Drives in Pensacola. Pensacola Historical Society photo.

Photography moved into the old barracks building.[4]

The city felt the social effects of the increased numbers of naval flight students both during the war and for years afterward. Just as their pre-war counterparts had, many fledgling naval aviators found Pensacola brides. In 1944 2,900 marriage licenses were issued in Escambia County, more than double the number issued in 1940.[5] The impact of these marriages was felt in later years when many of the aviators retired in Pensacola after their naval careers.

Pensacola's metropolitan population soared from 58,000 in 1940 to 77,000 in 1945.[6] A housing shortage soon developed and the people of Pensacola once again rented rooms and apartments to servicemen. The civilian population also contributed to the war effort by donating money to the War Fund Quota and the Community Chest. War bond

Volunteers for the United Service Organization posed with U. S. Navy Waves (Women Accepted For Volunteer Emergency Service) in front of the United Service Organization building on Spring Street in 1945. Pensacola Historical Society photo.

rallies were held and even school children bought ten cent stamps to fill an $18.50 book which would buy a $25.00 war bond.

Shortages of civilian goods soon developed as factories throughout the nation sold primarily to the armed forces. Tires were impossible to come by legally and gas for civilian usage was severely rationed. Pensacola teenagers were severely limited in the use of the family car because of gas rationing. Pensacola housewives coped with ration books when making up their grocery lists. Meat and sugar cost "ration points" and the number of points as well as the price of the commodity had to be taken into account by the housewife. Shoes were rationed and other items of civilian clothing were scarce as the nation's factories geared production toward the war effort.[7]

Many Pensacola women went to work for the first time in their lives. The U. S. Civil Service Commission actively recruited women to replace men in jobs aboard the Naval Air Station. The Assistant Secretary of the Navy issued a directive calling for increased training of women in occupations which had been traditionally reserved for men.[8] Women also took over their husbands' jobs as the men went to war. Mrs. Charles Blanchard ran the Pensacola Airport and Mrs. Edward P. Nickinson managed Merritt Shipping Agency.[9]

Other Pensacola women engaged in volunteer activities such as staffing the local USO or rolling bandages for the war effort. Even though these volunteers attempted to keep up the tradition of the "Southern Lady," they were proud of actually working for the war effort. Most of the volunteers had no plans for full time careers. In fact, the volunteers tended to disparage those women who actually worked for money; the paid workers, in turn, thought some of the volunteers were useless.[10] But, the seeds of social change were planted and the daughters and grand-daughters of these volunteers would later seek careers.[11]

The black population of Pensacola was most profoundly affected by the war. Servicemen from non-segregated areas of the country mingled with the local blacks. One result of this social inter-action was the formation, in 1942, of the Pensacola Improvement Association which was dedicated to educating blacks concerning voting rights. In 1943 more than 1,000 blacks were registered to vote, a large increase over previous years. Blacks entered the work force at the Naval Air Station in non-menial occupations. These social changes were just the beginning of the black movement in Pensacola.[12]

When the war ended, Pensacola was an altered city, larger and more cosmopolian than before. It had grown rich through the Navy's expansion and wanted to protect its new status. The Chamber of Commerce developed a three-pronged strategy: protect the naval bases; expand present industry; attract new industry. In the post-war years, Pensacolians were able to accomplish many of these goals.[13]

17 THE PAST IS PROLOGUE

The period following World War II was one of growth and expansion in Pensacola. Industrial plants opened; new suburbs were developed; education advanced with the opening of Pensacola Junior College and the University of West Florida; the Navy's role continued to be strong due to the necessity of training pilots for the Korean and Vietnam conflicts. The population continued to climb as a result of all these activities. By the decade of the 1980s the sleepy pre-war southern town had virtually disappeared to be replaced by a vibrant, growing city.

Modern industrial growth began when the Florida Pulp and Paper Company started its paper-making operation in Escambia County in 1939. World War II brought growth to the infant operation and soon after the war the local mill merged with St. Regis Paper Company and continued to grow and expand at its location in Cantonment. In the 1980s Champion International bought St. Regis and a new era in paper-making began.

In 1953 Chemstrand began making nylon fibers in a new plant just north of the city. Chemstrand became a wholly owned subsidiary of Monsanto in 1961 and in fifteen years employment at the plant tripled.[1]

These and other companies brought more people into Pensacola. An urgent need for more housing for this influx of both blue and white collar workers arose. In the 1950s the dream of Mary Ellison Baars to make Cordova Park, northeast of the city, an attractive place to live came true. In the years following, Cordova Park has been called the "quintessential suburb."[2]

Returning G. I.'s were one impetus to the founding of Pensacola Junior College which opened in 1948 in the old Aiken home on Palafox and Cervantes streets. The faculty and student body soon outgrew the house and in 1953 the college moved into the old Pensacola High School building on Lee Square. The college moved to its new, expanded campus near the airport in 1957.

As interest in local higher education grew, Pensacolians realized a need for a full-fledged university. The University of West Florida

The original home of Pensacola Junior College was in the old Aiken home at the intersection of Palafox and Cervantes Streets. Pensacola Historical Society photo taken in 1906.

Reubin O'Donovan Askew, born in Oklahoma in 1928, was nine when his family moved to Pensacola. A graduate of Pensacola High School and Florida State University, he served in the U. S. Air Force before obtaining his law degree from the University of Florida. Returning to Pensacola, he became assistant Escambia County solicitor. In 1958 he joined a Pensacola law firm and began a distinguished political career that carried him to the State Senate and the governor's office in 1970. He was the first governor to serve two full terms. He became one of Florida's most popular governors—frequently described as having presidential potential. He returned to public service serving as U. S. Trade Ambassador in President Jimmy Carter's administration. In 1984 he was among a large field of candidates seeking the Democratic party nomination for president. He subsequently began the practice of law in Miami. Interview with Jesse Earle Bowden, 1985. Pensacola Historical Society photo.

Daniel (Chappie) James, Jr., a native Pensacolian, was the first American black to attain the military rank of four-star general. Born in Pensacola in 1920, James grew up in a segregated neighborhood. His mother, Lillie A. James, operated a private school for black children, providing her youngest son, Chappie, with self-esteem and a grounding in basic education through the eighth grade. After graduation from the all black Washington High School in 1937, James attended Tuskegee University. Commissioned a second lieutenant in the U. S. Air Force in 1943 he achieved a remarkable record both as a combat pilot and as a fighter for racial equality. He saw action in Koren and Vietnam and later served as Commander of the North American Defense Force. He became the Pentagon's spokesman on American college campuses during Vietnam protests by students.

When he was promoted to four star general, James didn't mince words: "I got here because I'm dammed good. I filled all the squares." General James always counseled black students to obtain an education and to demonstrate a willingness to work to achieve prosperity. When he retired from the Air Force in 1978, he commented on the black situation in the United States, "We've still got another mile to run in the race for equality, but we've got a lot better track to run on and the trophies at the end are a lot better than they used to be." General Chappie James died three weeks after he retired. James R. McGovern, Black Eagle (University, Ala.: The University of Alabama Press, 1985). U. S. Air Force photo.

opened in the fall of 1967 as an upper-level institution. In the fall of 1983 the university admitted its first freshmen class and Pensacola now has a four-year university. Pensacola students may attend schools from kindergarten through graduate work in their own town. Both Pensacola Junior College and the University of West Florida also attract many students from other areas of Florida and the southeast.[3]

Pensacola's post-war growth brought problems, particularly erosion of the old downtown business district. When Town and Country Plaza opened in 1956, the flight of retail stores from Palafox Street began. In the early 1960s a small group of preservationists began the resurrection of the Seville Square area which had originally been platted by British surveyor Elias Durnford. The Pensacola Historical Society led the way with the establishment of the Pensacola Historical Museum in Old Christ Church. The city launched the restoration of the twenty-seven block area. The fledgling revitalization movement received added impetus when the Florida Legislature established the Historic Pensacola Preservation Board in 1967. Through the efforts of the Board and the Heritage Foundation, Seville Square rose from a downtrodden area to one of authentic Victorian charm. The North Hill Preservation Association inspired the restoration of the filligreed old homes that had degenerated into boarding houses. North Hill again stabilized and, once again, young families lived in the old houses. The old business district along Palafox Street was refurbished with restored old stores and brick sidewalks. As preservation continued to prosper in the 1970s, the city soon had three historic districts: Seville Square, North Hill and Palafox Place.

When new high-rise buildings began to dot Pensacola Beach, people became alarmed by the thought that another Miami Beach atmosphere with wall-to-wall hotels and condominiums would restrict access to the beach. The Gulf Islands National Seashore, established in 1971, brought the National Park Service to Pensacola. It preserved, in its natural state, fourteen miles of Santa Rosa Island and seven miles of Perdido Key. The white sands and blue waters of the Gulf remain accessible to all through this action. The woodlands of the old Naval Live Oaks Reservation also became part of the National Seashore. The Park Service supervised the restoration of old Forts Pickens and Barrancas, Battery San Antonio and the Redoubt and all of these forts are now open to visitors.[4]

During the 1980s downtown Pensacola has experienced a rennaissance. The new Pensacola Hilton Hotel, anchored to the restored

Interstate 110 snakes northward from downtown Pensacola past the new Hilton Hotel and the Civic Center. New construction along the waterfront is still changing the skyline of the old Port of Pensacola. Pensacola Historical Society photo.

1913 L & N Passenger Station, and the Pensacola Civic Center replaced a blighted area with a blend of old and new architecture. The restored 1925 Saenger Theater on Palafox Street serves as a community performing arts center. New government and private office buildings rise along the bayfront. Even though Pensacola residential areas are growing to the north and west of the old city, revitalization has attracted business and new residents to the once blighted inner city.

As in its long past, Pensacola still faces challenges and unsolved problems. The navy continues to employ the largest number of civilians in Escambia County making the city largely dependent upon the federal government for its economic well-being. A core of "rural thinking" people who are suspicious of change and distrustful of people who differ from them still resists threats of urban culture and "place a brake on

The Blue Angels, the U. S. Navy's Flight Demonstration Team, soar over the USS Lexington *moored to her pier at the Pensacola Naval Air Station. U. S. Navy photo.*

Pensacola's modernization in the post-war era."[5] Tourism is making a major move to become the number one industry of the area. Visitors are attracted to the historic sites: the forts, the museums and the restored houses. As long as the pure white sands beckon, tourists and natives will flock to the beaches and the waters that surround the old city.

For more than four centuries Pensacola has endured through hurricanes, fires, wars and changes of government. The old city of Anglo-Spanish origin remains a tenacious town, determined to preserve its long heritage as it enters the twenty-first century.

FOOTNOTES

1   "Many Canoes
Came to Greet Us"

¹An analysis of the sand showed it to be 99.65% silica. See James H. C. Martens, "Beaches of Florida," *21st-22nd Annual Report of the Florida State Geological Survey, 1982,*, 82; and Sandra Johnson, "Exhibit Notes for the Pensacola Historical Museum" (unpublished mss., 1984).

²Ibid.

³Ibid.

⁴See Jerald T. Milanich and Charles H. Fairbanks, *Florida Archaeology* (New York: Academic Press, Inc., 1980), 65; and Dianne Dusevitch, "Notes on Hawkshaw" (unpublished mss., 1985), Anthropology Department, University of West Florida.

⁵Johnson, "Exhibit Notes."

⁶Milanich and Fairbanks, *Florida Archaeology*, 193-94.

⁷Ibid.

⁸Louis B. Tesar, "Early History of Pensacola" (unpublished mss., n. d.), Pensacola Historical Museum, 10.

⁹Ibid.

¹⁰Ibid., 21-22; interview with Dr. William S. Coker, University of West Florida, Pensacola, Florida.

¹¹"Narrative of Alvar Nuñez Cabeça de Vaca," *Spanish Explorers in the Southern United States 1528-1543,* Frederick W. Hodge (ed.), (New York: Barnes and Noble, 1907), 40.

¹²Ibid., 38-39.

¹³Charles Hudson, Marvin Smith, David Hally, Richard Polhemus and Charles DePrater, "Coosa: A Chiefdom in the Sixteenth-Century Southeastern United States," *American Antiquity*, 50, no. 4 (Oct. 1985), 723-37.

¹⁴Theodore H. Lewis (ed.), "Narrative of the Expedition of Hernando De Soto by the Gentleman of Elvas," *Spanish Explorers in the Southern United States 1528-1543* (New York: Barnes and Noble, 1907), 183ff.

¹⁵Charles W. Arnade, "Tristan de Luna and Ochuse (Pensacola Bay) 1559" *Florida Historical Quarterly*, 37, nos. 3 & 4 (Jan.-Apr. 1954), 203.

2 "A Man Zealous In Our Time"

[1]Herbert Ingram Priestley, *Tristan de Luna, Conquistador of the Old South* (Glendale, Calif.: The Arthur H. Clark Co., 1963), 63.

[2]Ibid., 70.

[3]Ibid., 71.

[4]Ibid., 11.

[5]Herbert Ingram Priestly (ed.), *The Luna Papers: Documents Relating to the Expedition of Don Tristan de Luna y Arrellano for the conquest of La Florida in 1559-1561*, 2 vols. (Freeport, N. Y.: Books for Libraries Press, 1928; reprinted 1971), II, 212, 258.

[6]Ibid., II, 213.

[7]*The Luna Papers*, I, xxxv.

[8]*The Luna Papers*, II, 245.

[9]*The Luna Papers*,, I, 63.

[10]Priestley, *Tristan de Luna, Conquistador of the Old South*, 146.

[11]Ibid., 182.

3 "The Indians Call This Bay Panzacola"

[1]Irving A. Leonard, *Spanish Approach to Pensacola, 1689-1693*, Leonard (Albuquerque: The Quivira Society, 1939), 225.

[2]Albert Mauncy, "The Founding of Pensacola — Reasons and Reality," *Florida Historical Quarterly*, 37, nos. 3 & 4 (Jan.-Apr. 1959), 225-26.

[3]Leonard, *Spanish Approach to Pensacola*, 6-7.

[4]See ibid., 7-8; Mauncy, "The Founding of Pensacola," 227.

[5]William Edward Dunn, *Spanish and French Rivalry in the Gulf Region of the United States, 1678-1702* (Freeport, N. Y.: Books for Libraries Press, 1917), 105-106.

[6]Leonard, *Spanish Approach to Pensacola*, 12. Other theories as to how Pensacola got its name include: 1) it is a namesake of the Spanish town of Peniscola; 2) it is a corruption of the Spanish word for peninsula. Jordán's statement indicates that the town was named for the Panzacola Indians, a local tribe.

[7]"Sigüenza's Instructions and Journey," *Spanish Approach to Pensacola*, 154-55.

[8]Mauncy, "The Founding of Pensacola," 229.

[9]Stanley Faye, "Spanish Fortifications of Pensacola," *Florida Historical Quarterly*, 20, no. 2 (Oct. 1941), 151.

[10]"Sigüenza's Instructions and Journey," 160-61.

[11]Ibid., 162.

4   "The Finest Jewel"

[1]Irving A. Leonard, "Pensacola's First Spanish Period (1698-1763) Inception, Founding, and Troubled Existence," *Colonial Pensacola*, ed. by James R. McGovern (Pensacola: Pensacola-Escambia Development Commission, 1972), 7.

[2]Daniel Coxe, *A Description of the English Province of Carolina, By the Spaniards Called Florida, and by the French La Louisiane* (London, 1722; Facsimile Reproduction Gainesville: University Presses of Florida, 1976), xxii-xxx.

[3]See ibid.; *Spanish Approach to Pensacola, 1689-1693*. Translated with introduction by Irving A. Leonard (Albuquerque: The Quivira Society, 1939), 1.

[4]Albert Mauncy, "The Founding of Pensacola—Reasons and Reality," *Florida Historical Quarterly*, 37, nos. 3 & 4 (Jan.-Apr. 1959), 229-30.

[5]Ibid., 231.

[6]William S. Coker and C. Douglas Inglis, *The Spanish Censuses of Pensacola, 1784-1820: A Genealogical Guide to Spanish Pensacola* (Pensacola: The Perdido Bay Press, 1980), 61.

[7]Stanley Faye, "The Spanish Fortifications of Pensacola 1698-1821," *Florida Historical Quarterly*, 20, no. 2 (Oct. 1941), 152.

[8]Arriola to the King, 1 December 1698 as quoted in ibid., 153.

[9]William B. Griffen, "Spanish Pensacola 1700-1763," *Florida Historical Quarterly*, 37, nos. 3 & 4 (Jan.-Apr. 1959), 244.

[10]Ibid.

[11]Ibid.

[12]Ibid., 244-48.

[13]Ibid., 25.

[14]Faye, "Spanish Fortifications," 156.

5 "And Captured This Place . . ."

[1]See Stanley Faye, "The Contest For Pensacola Bay and Other Gulf Ports, 1698-1722," *Florida Historical Quarterly*, 24, no. 3 (Jan. 1946), 176-77; Charlton W. Tebeau, *A History of Florida* (Coral Gables, Fla.: University of Miami Press, 1971), 62.

[2]Faye, "Contest For Pensacola Bay," 189.

[3]James C. and Irene S. Coleman, *Guardians on the Gulf* (Pensacola: Pensacola Historical Society, 1982), 10.

[4]Faye, "Contest For Pensacola Bay," 184.

[5]Ibid., 206-207.

[6]Ibid., 66.

[7]Charlton W. Tebeau and Ruby Carson Leach, *Florida From Indian Trail to Space Age, A History* (Del Ray Beach: The Southern Publishing Co., 1965), 62.

[8]Faye, "Contest For Pensacola Bay," 317.

6 Storms And High Tides

[1]Stanley Faye, "Spanish Fortifications of Pensacola, 1698-1763," *Florida Historical Quarterly*, 20, no. 2 (Oct. 1941), 160.

[2]Ibid., 162.

[3]Charlton W. Tebeau, *History of Florida*(Coral Gables: University of Miami Press, 1971), 66-67.

[4]William S. Coker, "The Financial History of Pensacola's Spanish Presidios 1698-1763," *Pensacola Historical Society Quarterly*, IX, no. 4 (Spring 1979), 6-7.

[5]Tebeau, *History of Florida*, 67.

[6]Coker, "Financial History," 5.

[7]Stanley Faye, "Spanish and British Fortifications of Pensacola 1698-1821," *Florida Historical Quarterly*, 20, no. 3 (Jan. 1942), 164.

7   His Majesty's Loyal Colony

[1]Quoted in Robert Gold, *Borderland Empires in Transition, The triple Nation Transfer of Florida* (Carbondale and Edwardsville: Southern Illinois University Press, 1959), 19.

[2]Quoted in Cecil Johnson, "Pensacola in the British Period: Summary and Significance," *Florida Historical Quarterly*, 38, nos. 3 & 4 (Jan.-Apr. 1959), 265.

[3]*Mississippi Provincial Archives 1763-1766, English Dominion*, compiled and edited by Dunbar Rowland (Nashville: Press of Brandon Printing Co., 1911), I, 113.

[4]Gold, *Borderland Empires*, 122.

[5]Ibid., 57-58.

[6]Charlton W. Tebeau, *A History of Florida* (Coral Gables: University of Miami Press, 1971), 81.

[7]Johnson, "Pensacola in the British Period," 264.

[8]For a complete account of the British government in West Florida, see Robert R. Rae and Milo B. Howard, Jr., *The Minutes, Journals and Acts of the General Assembly* (University, Ala.: University of Alabama Press, 1976).

[9]Cecil Johnson, *British West Florida 1763-1783* (Yale University Press, 1942; reprinted by Archon Books, 1971), 43.

[10]Ibid., 43-45.

[11]Ibid., 60.

[12]Ibid., 69.

[13]Ibid., 75-81, 114.

[14]Ibid., 205.

[15]For a complete account of the Battle of Mobile, See William S. Coker and Hazel P. Coker, *The Siege of Mobile 1780 in Maps with Data on Troop Strength, Military Units, Ships, Casualties, and Prisoners of War including a brief history of Fort Charlotte (Condé)*, Vol. IX in The Spanish Borderlands Series (Pensacola: The Perdido Bay Press, 1982).

[16]Elizabeth Vickers, "A Talk to the Daughters of the American Revolution, March 13, 1985" (unpublished mss., Pensacola Historical Museum).

[17]For a complete account of the siege, see *Siege! Spain and Britain: Battle of Pensacola March 9-May 8, 1781*, edited by Virginia Parks

(Pensacola: Pensacola Historical Society, 1981); also William S. Coker and Hazel P. Coker, *The Siege of Pensacola, 1781, in Maps with Data on Troops Strength, Military Units, Ships, Casualties, and Related Statistics*, Vol. VIII in The Spanish Borderlands Series (Pensacola: The Perdido Bay Press, 1981).

8 SUNSET OF AN EMPIRE

[1]L. N. McAlister, "Pensacola During the Second Spanish Period," *Florida Historical Quarterly*, 37, nos. 3 and 4 (Jan.-Apr. 1959), 288-90.

[2]Frank L. Mayes, "Pensacola and its Environs," *Bliss Quarterly*, III, no. 3 (Pensacola, Jan. 1897), 10; and interview with Dr. William S. Coker.

[3]J. A. Brown, "Panton, Leslie and Company, Indian Traders of Pensacola and St. Augustine," *Florida Historical Quarterly*, 37, nos. 3 & 4 (Jan.-Apr. 1959), 301.

[4]John Walton Caughey, *McGillivray of the Creeks* (Norman: University of Oklahoma Press, 1938), 24.

[5]William S. Coker, *et al.*, *John Forbes' Description of the Spanish Floridas, 1804* (Pensacola: The Perdido Bay Press, 1979), 35. For an in depth study of Panton, Leslie and Company, see William S. Coker and Thomas D. Watson, *Indian Traders of the Southeastern Spanish Borderlands* (Gainesville: University Presses of Florida, 1985).

[6]McAlister, "Second Spanish Period," 301.

[7]Ibid.

[8]Caughey, *McGillivrary of the Creeks*, 44ff.

[9]Ibid., 53.

[10]See Coker, *Forbes' Description*, 6; Coker and Watson, *Indian Traders*, 226-329.

[11]Charlton W. Tebeau, *A History of Florida* (Coral Gables: University of Miami Press, 1971), 97.

[12]McAlister, "Second Spanish Period," 309.

[13]William S. Coker and G. Douglas Inglis, *The Spanish Censuses of Pensacola, 1784-1820: A Genealogical Guide to Spanish Pensacola* (Pensacola: The Perdido Bay Press, 1980), 6.

[14]Ibid., 14.

[15]Ibid., 7-9.

9   "Scalp For Scalp"

[1]Isaac J. Cox, *The West Florida Controversy, 1778-1813* (Baltimore: Johns Hopkins Press, 1918), 85ff.

[2]William S. Coker, "Andrew Jackson, the Spanish Floridas and the United States," in *Andrew Jackson and Pensacola*, edited by James R. McGovern (Pensacola: The Jackson Day Sesquicentennial Committee, 1971), 40.

[3]Ibid.

[4]See Stanley Faye, "The British and Spanish Foritfications of Pensacola," *Florida Historical Quarterly*, 20, no. 3 (Jan. 1942), 288; Coker, "Andrew Jackson," 40-41.

[5]Coker, "Andrew Jackson," 42.

[6]Ibid., 43.

[7]Samuel Flagg Bemis, *John Quincy Adams and the Foundations of American Foreign Policy* (New York: Alfred A. Knopf, 1956), 300ff.

[8]Marquis James, *Andrew Jackson The Border Captain* (New York: Garden City Publishing Co., Inc., 1940)

[9]Quoted in Coker, "Andrew Jackson," 45.

[10]Marquis James, *The Life of Andrew Jackson* (Indianapolis: The Bobbs-Merrill Co., 1938), 318.

10   "Such A Mixed Multitude"

[1]Quoted in William S. Coker and G. Douglas Inglis, *The Spanish Censuses of Pensacola, 1784-1820: A Genealogical Guide to Spanish Pensacola* (Pensacola: The Perdido Bay Press, 1980), 7.

[2]"A letter by Rachel Jackson," published in *Andrew Jackson and Pensacola*, ed. by James R. McGovern (Pensacola: The Jackson Day Sesquicentennial Commission, 1971), 31-34.

[3]William S. Coker, "Andrew Jackson, The Spanish Floridas and the United States," *Andrew Jackson and Pensacola*, ed. by James R. McGovern (Pensacola: Jackson Day Sesquicentennial Commission, 1971), 46.

[4]Ibid., 47.

[5]Sidney Walter Martin, *Florida During the Territorial Days* (Athens: University of Georgia Press, 1944), 23.

[6]Ibid.

[7]Ibid., 167.

[8]Ibid., 165.

[9]Coker, "Andrew Jackson," 48.

[10]Herbert J. Doherty, Jr., "Ante-Bellum Pensacola: 1821-1860," *Florida Historical Quarterly* 37, nos. 3 & 4 (Jan.-Apr. 1959), 343.

[11]Andrew Jackson to George Walton, 26 November 1822, quoted in *Florida Historical Quarterly* 34, no. 1 (July 1954), 26.

[12]Elizabeth D. Vickers, "The Golden Dream, Life in Pensacola in the 1870s," *Pensacola Historical Society Quarterly* VII, no. 3 (Spring 1974), 19.

[13]Charlton W. Tebeau, *A History of Florida* (Coral Gables: University of Miami Press, 1971), 122.

[14]George F. Pearce, *The U. S. Navy in Pensacola* (Gainesville: University Presses of Florida, 1980), 6.

[15]Quoted in ibid., 9-10.

[16]Ibid., 16.

[17]William F. Keller, "Henry Marie Brackenridge First United States Forester," *Forest History* (Jan. 1972), 12-23.

[18]Virginia Parks, "The Naval Live Oak Reservation," *Pensacola Historical Society Quarterly* (Spring 1975), 2-10.

[19]Ibid., 21.

[20]James C. and Irene S. Coleman, *Guardians on the Gulf* (Pensacola: Pensacola Historical Society, 1982), 35-36.

[21]Ibid., 34-35.

[22]Jesse Earle Bowden, "Canal Dreams and Railroad Reality," *Iron Horse in the Pinelands*, ed. by Virginia Parks (Pensacola: Pensacola Historical Society, 1982), 8-11.

[23]Martin, *Florida During the Territorial Days*, 265-76.

11   "THOSE ARCADIAN DAYS"

[1]John McIntosh Kell, *Recollections of a Naval Life* (Washington, D. C.: 1900), quoted in Ernest F. Dibble *Antebellum Pensacola and the Military Presence* (Pensacola: Pensacola/Escambia County Development Commission, 1974), 13.

[2]James Knox Polk, "Pensacola Commerce and Industry 1821-1860," (Master's Thesis, University of West Florida, 1971), 83-84.

118

³Ibid., 85, 97.

⁴Ibid., 46-65.

⁵George F. Pearce, "Torment of Pestilence: Yellow Fever Epidemics in Pensacola," *Florida Historical Quarterly*, 56, no. 4 (Apr. 1978), 454.

⁶William M. Straight, "The Yellow Jack," *The Journal of the Florida Medical Association* 58, no. 8 (August 1971), 35.

⁷Pearce, "Torment of Pestilence," 455.

⁸Dibble, *Antebellum Pensacola and the Military Presence*, 85.

⁹Ibid., 138-39. The phrase, "Judas burnings," refers to the practice of making a effigies of Juda Iscariot at the beginning of Lent. The effigies were burned on the day before Easter. The custom originated in Spain and was probably brought to Pensacola during the last Spanish period. See Catherine L. Stewart and Maude Hollowell, *Old Customs of Pensacola and Favorite Recipes of the Times* (Pensacola: Historic Pensacola Preservation Society, 1974), 3.

12   TO EXILE AND BACK

¹Quoted in George F. Pearce, *The U. S. Navy in Pensacola* (Pensacola: University Presses of Florida, 1980), 66.

²Adam Ricks and Norman Simons, "Pensacola in the Civil War," *Pensacola Historical Society Quarterly* IX, no. 2 (Spring 1978), 11.

³Edwin C. Bearss, "Civil War Operations In and Around Pensacola," *Florida Historical Quarterly* 36, no. 1 (July 1957), 125.

⁴Slemmer to the War Department, *War of the Rebellion: Official Records of the Union and Confederate Armies*, Ser. 1, Vol. I (Washington: Government Printing Office, 1890-1911), 334.

⁵Ibid.

⁶Rick and Simons, "Pensacola in the Civil War," 12-15.

⁷Ibid., 16.

⁸Ibid.

⁹Ibid., 17-18.

¹⁰Ibid., 18.

¹¹Ibid., 19.

¹²Leora Sutton, *The Walton House* (Pensacola: Privately Published, 1968), 41.

¹³Woodward B. Skinner, "Pensacola's Exiled Government," *Florida Historical Quarterly* 39, no. 3 (January 1961), 270-73.

[14]William Watson Davis, *The Civil War and Reconstruction in Florida* (New York, 1913), 307.

[15]Earle Bowden, "Asboth Finds City Deserted: Shack Town Emerges Here; Moreno Protests," *Pensacola News Journal*, 29 September 1963.

[16]Leora Sutton, *Pensacola in 1868* (Pensacola, n.d.).

[17]Alice P. Kenney, "Exile to the Ends of the Earth," *Pensacola History Illustrated*, 1, no. 2 (Pensacola: Pensacola Historical Society, 1984), 3.

[18]*Florida in the Civil War — 1860 Through Reconstruction* (Pensacola: Civil War Round Table of Pensacola, 1961), 57.

[19]Quoted in Kenney, "Exile to the Ends of the Earth," 3.

13   Boom Town

[1]Jesse Earle Bowden, "Colonel Chipley Builds a Railroad," *Iron Horse in the Pinelands* (Pensacola: Pensacola Historical Society, 1982), 22-36.

[2]Quoted in ibid., 31.

[3]Bowden, "Canal Dreams and Railroad Reality," 13.

[4]Frank J. Oaks, "The Port of Pensacola 1877-1920," unpublished mss., 1970, Leilia Abercrombie Library, Pensacola Historical Museum, 1-8.

[5]Richard Massey, Jr. "A History of the Lumber Industry in Alabama and West Florida, 1880-1914," unpublished mss., Historic Pensacola Preservation Board, 18.

[6]Ibid., 62.

[7]Quoted in Lucius and Linda Ellsworth, *Pensacola The Deep Water City* (Tulsa: Continental Heritage Press, Inc., 1982), 66.

[8]Occie Clubbs, "Pensacola in Retrospect," *Florida Historical Quarterly* 37, nos. 3 & 4 (Jan.-Apr. 1959), 379-81.

[9]Ballast is defined as any heavy material such as sand or gravel which is placed in a ship's hold to sink her to such a depth as to prevent her from capsizing when in motion. The term "in ballast" means that a ship is loaded with ballast. It is not a saleable or paying cargo.

[10]Interview with Elizabeth Vickers.

[11]Letter Stephen S. Leonard to Dr. Joseph Y. Podree, State Health

Officer, 27 March 1900, in *15th Annual Report of the State Board of Health-1901*, 81.

[12]Circuit Court Cast 1878-8060, Archives Division, Escambia County Judicial Center, "Barcelona Street Wharf Company."

[13]Modeste Hargis, "Escambia County History." Ruth B. Barr (ed.) (Pensacola: WPA, Federal Writers Project, 1936), 55.

[14]James R. McGovern, *The Emergence of a City In The Modern South: Pensacola 1900-1945* (DeLeon Springs, Fla.: E. O. Painter Printing Co., 1976), 180.

[15]Ted Carrageorge, "The Greeks of Pensacola" *Ethnic Minorities in Gulf Coast Society*, Jerrell H. Shofner and Linda V. Ellsworth (eds.) (Pensacola: Gulf Coast History and Humanities Conference, 1979), VIII, 56-68.

[16]McGovern, *Emergence of a City*, 6.

[17]Donald H. Bragaw, "Loss of Identity," *Florida Historical Quarterly* 51, no. 4, 414-18.

[18]Ellsworth, *Deep Water City*, 74.

[19]Donald H. Bragaw, "Status of Negroes in a Southern Port City in the Progressive Era: Pensacola 1896-1920," *Florida Historical Quarterly* 50, no. 4, 261-303.

[20]Charlene Hunter, "A History of Pensacola's Black Community," unpublished mss., Special Collections, John C. Pace Library, University of West Florida, Pensacola, Florida.

[21]Pensacola City Directories 1893-94 and 1905.

[22]McGovern, *Emergence of a City*, 16-18.

[23]Ibid.

[24]George F. Pearce, *The U. S. Navy in Pensacola* (Pensacola: University Presses of Florida, 1980), 108.

[25]Quoted in Gloria Jahoda, *The Other Florida* (New York: Charles Scribner's Sons, 1967), 48.

14 THE MOTHER-IN-LAW OF THE NAVY

[1]D. Douglas Davis and Elizabeth Vickers, "Fort Barrancas 1875," *Pensacola Historical Society Quarterly* (Summer 1974), 7-10.

[2]George F. Pearce, *The U. S. Navy in Pensacola* (Pensacola: University Presses of Florida, 1980), 98.

[3]Ibid., 111.

[4]Ibid.

[5]James C. and Irene S. Coleman, *Guardians on the Gulf* (Pensacola: Pensacola Historical Society, 1982), 53, 71.

[6]Pearce, *U. S. Navy in Pensacola*, 113-25.

[7]Harold B. Harden and Kendrick T. Ford, "The Increased Naval Activity at Pensacola, Florida, 1914-1919, and Its Influence Upon Pensacola's Economy and Culture," pamphlet in Special Collections, John C. Pace Library, University of West Florida, Pensacola, Florida.

[8]Quoted in Pearce, *U. S. Navy in Pensacola*, 132.

[9]*Pensacola Journal*, 10 December 1923.

[10]Pearce, *U. S. Navy in Pensacola*, 161.

[11]James R. McGovern, *The Emergence of a City in the Modern South: Pensacola 1900-1945* (DeLeon Springs, Fla.: E. O. Painter Printing Co., 1976), 30.

[12]Janice Croft, "A Twin Success Story: Pensacola and Newport," pamphlet, Leilia Abercrombie Library, Pensacola Historical Museum, 6.

15 THE ROARING TWENTIES AND DEPRESSING THIRTIES

[1]James R. McGovern, *The Emergence of a City in the Modern South: Pensacola 1900-1945* (DeLeon Springs, Fla.: E. O. Painter Printing Co., 1976), 209n3. Chapter VI gives a complete and interesting account of Pensacola in the 1920s and most of the material for this section has come from Dr. McGovern's book.

[2]Ibid., 81.

[3]Ibid., 90-93.

[4]Ibid., 93.

[5]Personal interview with Marion Raby, 1979.

[6]McGovern, *Emergence of a City*, 119.

[7]Ibid., 127.

[8]Quoted in ibid., 130.

[9]Ibid., 220n153.

[10]Ibid., 132.

[11]James C. and Irene S. Coleman, *Guardians on the Gulf* (Pensacola: Pensacola Historical Society, 1982), 77.

16   War Changes The City

[1]James R. McGovern, *The Emergence of a City in the Modern South: Pensacola 1900-1945* (DeLeon Springs, Fla.: E. O. Painter Printing Co., 1976), 153. FDR was, of course, President Franklin Delano Roosevelt. The "dastardly deed" was the phrase Roosevelt used to describe the attack on Pearl Harbor in his speech to Congress on December 8, 1941.

[2]Ibid., 153-54.

[3]Ibid., 154-55.

[4]Interview with Colonel Richard B. Olney, United States Air Force (Retired). Colonel Olney was a second lieutenant attached to the regimental staff of the Thirteenth Coast Artillery in 1941.

[5]McGovern, *Emergence of a City*, 160.

[6]Norman Simons and James R. McGovern, *Pensacola in Pictures and Print* (Pensacola: The Pensacola Series Commemorating the American Revolution Bicentennial, 1974), IV, 130.

[7]Personal recollections of the author and of Harriet Major.

[8]Assistant Secretary of the Navy to All Naval and Marine Corps Activities Concerned (ALNAV) 26 June 1941, NAS Library, NAS Pensacola, Fla.

[9]McGovern, *Emergence of a City*, 164.

[10]Interview with Mary Riley Veal.

[11]McGovern, *Emergence of a City*, 164.

[12]Ibid., 167.

[13]Ibid., 170.

17   The Past Is Prologue

[1]John Appleyard Agency, *An Industrial History of Pensacola* (Pensacola: The Pensacola Home and Savings Association, 1970).

[2]Lucius and Linda Ellsworth, *Pensacola the Deep Water City* (Tulsa: Continental Heritage Press, 1982), 154.

[3]Ibid., 178.

[4]Jesse Earle Bowden, "Pensacola History: Where the Past Is Prologue," (speech to the Pensacola Rotary Club, October 19, 1979).

[5]James R. McGovern, *The Emergence of a City in the Modern South: Pensacola 1900-1945* (DeLeon Springs, Fla.: E. O. Painter Printing Co., 1976), 154.

INDEX